STING
LIKE A BEE

STING LIKE A BEE

THE MUHAMMAD ALI STORY

JOSÉ TORRES

AND BERT RANDOLPH SUGAR

PREFACE BY NORMAN MAILER | EPILOGUE BY BUDD SCHULBERG

Contemporary Books

Chicago   New York   San Francisco   Lisbon   London   Madrid   Mexico City
Milan   New Delhi   San Juan   Seoul   Singapore   Sydney   Toronto

Library of Congress Cataloging-in-Publication Data
CIP information is on file with the Library of Congress.

Contemporary Books 🖉

A Division of The McGraw·Hill Companies

1 2 3 4 5 6 7 8 9 0   AGM/AGM   0 9 8 7 6 5 4 3 2 1

99- 88560mm

ISBN 0-07-139588-1
B
ALI,
This book was set in Sabon
Printed and bound by Quebecor Martinsburg
muHAmmAD

Cover design by Nick Panos
Cover photograph copyright © Allsport Hulton Deutsch/Allsport
Interior design by Nick Panos

To
Andrés Torres, Sr. and Cus D'Amato

CONTENTS

PART III

PREFACE
BY
NORMAN MAILER

Anyone who knows prizefighters and does not have to make his living by writing about them too often, knows that they are usually intelligent men. Of course, the worst of them get deadened in their intelligence—it is not that what they say is stupid, but they have blank spots. In the process of reasoning from A to B then to C and to D, they are likely to miss a couple of letters. Their brains get damaged from punches, but essentially in the way a good engine whose spark plugs are gone will sound spotty in its timing. The popular assumption that professional boxers do not have brains comes from sportswriters (but then sportswriters' brains are in their turn damaged by the obligation to be clever each day). The quantities of booze necessary to lubricate such racing of the mental gears ends up giving the sportswriters the equivalent of a good many punches to the head. So most of them duck their task. They do not try to comprehend fighters. They prefer to treat them in tried and true ways, as rather heroic but silly fellows, or as clowns with a penchant for offbeat or gnomic remarks. It makes good copy, and it satisfies

the average man who finds it bad enough after all that these boxers could take him in a street fight without having to swallow the
added gall that boxers might be smarter as well. The fact that
fighters who become champions are most intelligent men with a
marvelous sense of balance in their estimate of changing events
under high pressure is an idea so painful, that it doesn't even get
whispered about. Nonetheless, it is true—champions are most
intelligent men—and the reason so many of the remarks of
Muhammad Ali and Sonny Liston and Floyd Patterson, of Sugar
Ray Robinson, and Jake LaMotta and Rocky Graziano, of Carmen Basilio and Joe Frazier and Rocky Marciano and Gene
Fullmer all sound so peculiar in print is that their original words
were usually economical, astute, and cut into the middle of what
was absurd in a particular situation. But the occasion was poorly
reported, the remark (usually obscene) was cleaned off in the old
dishwater of copy desk good taste, and the point was invariably
shifted to another point which was less interesting. All those
sportswriters punch drunk on twenty years of booze! So fighters, full of instinctive metaphor, come through like bugs who
speak. It is as if we insist that athletes who are great in the ring
should have for civilized balance no real stature outside.

The fact that boxers do not often write books does nothing to
dispel the illusion that they are stupid. Indeed when they have
their name on books, we all know they do not write them—they
have ghostwriters or collaborators who may be kind enough to
ask them questions once in a while. In fact, the only book by a
good boxer which may actually have been done by the boxer was
a work by Gene Tunney which I remember reading in *The Saturday Evening Post* many years ago. It was a memoir and a
courtly one, and I have no idea today how much of it truly
belonged to Tunney. It may have been completely ghostwritten
for all I know, but it is the only work I can remember, outside of

the one you are now holding in your hands, which could have been genuinely composed by a fighter.

This one, now before you, was written by José Luis "Cheqüi" Torres. It may be the first such book of its kind. I can testify to the truth of that, or at least of the genuineness of at least half of this book, Parts I and III, because José wrote those parts over a month of the hardest work in June of 1971 up in Vermont while living near me, and I saw the pages done each day, and functioned as a sort of editor each night, suggesting cuts, and giving Torres a fatherly hand with verb tenses from time to time. In its quiet way, I thought the book was a modest phenomenon for it was being written by a man who had been a Light Heavyweight Champion for a couple of years and had had no more education than other fighters, and had learned to speak and to think and to write in Spanish first, and had picked up his English with some pain, and was still, as you can see by the prose, not absolutely comfortable with it, yet I preferred to edit with a light hand and leave alone most of his odd and sometimes strained or over-formal phrasings for the flavor of his thought and attitude—which were essentially Spanish—are in it. So it is his book—I can swear to that. He wrote Parts I and III working six to ten hours a day all through a hot month of June, and succeeded there I think in offering a view of boxing which comes for the first time, genuinely and authentically from the inside.

Part II is another matter. Part II is a book more like other books which are about prizefighting and about Muhammad Ali, and while I am obviously not as fond of Part II, the middle of this book, as I am of its beginning and end, I think that for readers who love sports pages, there are a good many amusing anecdotes here, and plenty of new interviews, as well as that air of the quaint (at a comfortably low literary level) which people expect when they read a feature story on a sports page. This part of the book was a collaboration and was written by José Torres *and* Bert Sugar, the publisher of *Boxing Illustrated*. While it is true that Torres did much of the actual writing in Part II, Sugar did all the research except for the interviews (which were Torres'), and so the flavor of the material was gathered more through the eyes, senses, and literary instincts of a professional sportswriter than a prizefighter. Therefore, Part II, while it is likely to please many readers of this book more than Parts I and III, precisely because it is more familiar in its approach to boxing legends, does keep the merits of *Sting Like a Bee* down on the literary farm. For the mystery of Ali's personality, while thoroughly amplified for us in Part II, is never brought closer to explanation.

Still, what we are given in Parts I and III is considerable, and makes of this book a subtly impressive event. We are brought for the first time into the ring through the eyes of a man who has been a great boxer himself. So we suddenly see fights not as we are accustomed to look at them in the pages of books, but as intellectual and characterological struggles between highly skilled artists. Or if the notion of boxers-as-artists is banal by now, then at least we see them as highly skilled human machines of will and ingenuity and *strategy*. What impresses us about boxing, the blood and the pain and the stamina, are merely the given conditions to Torres. He takes them for granted, is concerned with them no more than a chess master would bother to annotate the headaches and eyestrain of a long match. No, it is the intellectual content of a fight which absorbs him. The problems and the mysterious solution to some of these problems capture him, and a continuing inquiry runs through his mind.

It is founded on the very old argument between instinct and reason. He is obsessed with that. Torres was trained by Cus D'Amato, the only prizefight manager remotely comparable to a

Scholastic. D'Amato is a manager so unlike that common view of prizefight managers as leeches, parasites and thieves that he seems to find it obscene if any of his boys get hit, and indeed over the years D'Amato has worked out such a master schedule of thrust and riposte, of block and slip and counter to every conceivable punch and combination of punches that one might have to turn to Clausewitz for a view of warfare as elaborated and comprehensive. Torres was his prize pupil—perhaps even more gifted instinctively, and certainly through training, than Floyd Patterson, for Torres, unlike Patterson, was, during his prime, almost impossible to hit (perhaps because he did not have Patterson's love of the immolating flame). Indeed, at his prime, José Torres was a phenomenal fighting machine. He had the speed of a fast middleweight, even of a fast welterweight, and he could hit as hard as any heavyweight. He could knock out his opponents with a left hook or a straight right, he had a jab so fine he could out-jab Willie Pastrano, who had no real punch other than the best jab in the business, and moreover, Torres had all the impregnable defenses D'Amato had designed for years, and always boxed with his gloves protecting his head, and could slip punches with both fists up as well as Cassius Clay could then slip punches with both hands down. There were a few people in boxing who could be heard to say that if José Torres had the desire, there was no reason he could not have become the greatest boxer in the history of the game and it is true (at the very least in this writer's belief) that Torres was the only man around in those years, in the prime of Muhammad Ali when Ali was winning monotonous contests with men like Chuvalo, Mildenberger, Zora Folley and Terrell, who could have given Ali a terrible night and could conceivably have beaten him, for he was as fast as Ali or faster, and hit as hard or harder, and was very difficult to find in a ring, just as difficult as Ali. Why then did he end with no more than the high, fine honors of being light heavyweight champion of his time with a most respectable record of three successful title defenses before he lost his crown to an older fighter, Dick Tiger?

The answer could take a book. It is buried in those enigmas which surround the question of why a man with the talent of a genius does not become a genius. But in brief, the answer could rest in the thought that Torres did not have the kind of hunger which drives men to transcendence. Ali, most mysteriously, does not seem to have had that hunger either, unless the flaming orbits of his ego were powered by a fuel of desperation we cannot even begin to conceive. For certain, however, Ali had one huge flood tide in his favor—the cause of his own black people—and he has always been the most extraordinary pilot of our time as he has floated the boat of his iron-and-eggshell ego down that collective river of black instinct which is approaching the headwaters of their liberation. No current, once attached to it, can be more powerful. Whereas Torres, like you or me, is a man alone who works on the smaller tides of his own appetites, vanities, imperatives, anxieties and pride. So I do not know if he would have beaten Ali if they had both met at their peak, for Ali might have found a thousand ways to weaken José psychologically before the bell, but of this I can be certain—that the mystery of Ali's attachment to boxing as a deep function of the human instinct has produced a book in a man brought up uniquely as was Torres by boxing reason, which any lover of prizefighting will read and read again in favorite parts and say, "This Puerto Rican is fantastic. He was good enough to be champion and now he's written a book which, Goddammit, makes me think I never knew there was that much to boxing."

As for Torres' personality, well, he is my friend, so why weaken friendship by talking of his virtues? Suffice it that when his Afro is in shape and he is listening seriously to a new acquaintance who has something interesting to say, why then he has the dignity and most impressive mien of a serious revolutionary or judge. Then, you desire his good opinion. And when he is laughing at something just said which he thinks funny, why then he pounds the table with his fingertips, and laughs in a high and uncontrollable voice, and often as not falls on the floor. He is that much out of control! The night we became friends, he had knocked out Bobo Olson in the first round at the Garden and was finally on his way to becoming champion. I had invited him and his wife and a couple of their friends out to dinner; I was acting, I suppose, like a rich fight buff jumping on to take care of an up-and-coming fighter. So, Torres, assuming no doubt he ought to sing a little for his supper, looked at me solemnly at one point during the meal and said, "You keep in good condition?"

"You kidding?" I asked.

And he fell out of his chair laughing. Right at Toots Shor's. It is his greatest charm. Anybody can knock him down in conversation with an honest line. It is probably because as he puts it, "Boxers are liars," and he was able to lie so well in the ring. What is remarkable now is the huge distance he has come against the deepest habits of prevarication in himself, those habits every good boxer knows from his childhood's bones. For to be honest is to get hit, yes, what a distance José has come to work now at writing, to work at that game where the rewards are given for that truth you've elucidated from the tricky memories of the flesh. *Andale, hombre!* I am waiting for your next book. If you get better than good, Cheqüi, maybe I will become the best late-middle-aged boxer in the literary world, and that is a small honor to all but a working writer in the core of his prime.

ABOUT THE AUTHORS

A silver medalist in the 1956 Olympics, JOSÉ TORRES went on to have a brilliant professional boxing career, becoming light-heavyweight champion of the world in 1965. After his fighting days ended, Torres became a columnist for the *New York Post* and associate editor of *Boxing Illustrated* magazine. From 1983 to 1988 he served as chairman of the New York State Boxing Commission. He publishes regularly in *Parade*, the *New York Post*, *El Diario*, and the *Village Voice* and is the author of *Fire and Fear: The Inside Story of Mike Tyson*. He lives in New York City.

BERT RANDOLPH SUGAR is a sports pundit, raconteur, and author of over fifty books. He has founded two boxing magazines and appears frequently on television to discuss the sport, always clad in his trademark fedora and smoking a large cigar. Bert lives in Chappaqua, New York, and is currently writing a book on the Boston Red Sox–New York Yankees rivalry.

PART I

CHAPTER 1

Muhammad Ali: Was there always a band traveling in his wake as he rolled through the cities of the Sixties? A prince of his time and one of the great artists of the instrument known as the media. If you were alive during his time, you knew about him. Knew the handsome face, knew the voice moving from loudness to mock modesty in a kind of irony. He was American in a way that few others were American, because in him there was always the possibility of tragedy. He was a romantic, a man who believed in possibilities; if you believed hard enough, you could become the Olympic champion, the world's heavyweight champ, you could have the expensive houses, the Cadillacs, and you could do it all without losing anything, without compromising, without being damaged, without being hurt.

Muhammad Ali: black prince. His dignity always with him. And when it seemed to end on the night when he finally lost his championship, there was a sign in the 125th Street Station of the A train in New York. It said, quite simply, "Ali lives."

October 25, 1970. The day before the Ali–Quarry fight. It is almost midnight. The streets of Atlanta are quiet. The people who work in the fancy stores on Peachtree Street have vanished to the suburbs and we are in a wild and laughing knot of human beings coming out of a Loew's movie house as if they are part of a parade. At the head is a tall, good-looking man who is obviously the leader. His name: Muhammad Ali.

"That's right, man," he yells to the crowd. "The real champ is gonna show the world who is the greatest. So get to the fight early. The man might fall in one."

"What round, Ali?" someone asks, as if they listen to him but don't listen to him.

He starts to shadowbox and the crowd steps back to watch. "I'm feeling better than ever," he screams. "Better than ever."

"I hear that the fight won't take place," says a young girl. "Will you be disappointed?"

"Ask Jerry Quarry," Ali says. "I'm used to worse things."

Now we are at the Ali–Quarry fight headquarters at the ultramodern Regency-Hyatt House Hotel. "Here I am," he yells extending both arms as if to embrace the heavens. "The king is here." Smiles. "You see that," he says, pointing to the largely black crowd, "That's my people coming in from all over the country. Came to see the king . . . the real champion."

Blacks move through the lobby of the Regency-Hyatt. They are wearing multi-colored outfits. Some have rims on their hats so large they look like small umbrellas. They have arrived in psychedelic-colored Cadillacs, Mercedes-Benzes, Rolls Royces. Some are equipped with white chauffeurs. Blond whores from New York and from Chicago walk hand-in-hand with their rich, black pimps, displaying super-mini skirts. Their cars are comfortably double-parked on the streets of Atlanta.

Black language reverberates all over the city that Scarlet O'Hara once knew, the city that is now 51 percent black. Blacks are still arriving at the nation's fourth busiest airport by way of seven airlines. They are coming in on the seven bus lines that serve Atlanta. Many of the rich ones who are afraid to fly, or apprehensive of the long drives, sent their chauffeurs with their cars and travel instead by one of the thirteen rail lines.

In the middle of the hotel lobby is a bar which looks like a giant seashell suspended in the air. It's the fanciest hotel I've ever seen. The language of the place is special. "Man, we own this place," says Ali, regarding the parade of blacks in the lobby. Some of the laughter is wild. As a black from Watts says, some of the people are talking "Harlem language." Throughout the week preceding the fight the Southern whites, who ran the bar, were puzzled by the blacks with the fancy clothes. "We can't allow no one here without a tie," said a bartender to a young black from New York.

"You just," he was told, "can't wear a tie with *this* outfit. C'mon, my man, don't spoil my fashion."

Now people are drinking without being worried about ties or jackets. "You know," someone tells Ali, "the hotel changed the rules. We don't need special clothes anymore."

Now after three-and-a-half years of such inactivity, still engaged in a series of legal wrangles, most of his money gone and, with prison facing him, his name a synonym for controversy, Muhammad Ali is coming back. Walking with him in the Atlanta night, it is still difficult to believe, even for Ali himself.

"I'm thinking about this fight," he says more than once. "I need the money and I need security for my family. I don't want to spoil this fight by getting involved politically. I'm a fighter, period." But it is hard for Ali to keep away from the political vibrations that fill the air every time he holds a press conference. It is common knowledge that the fight is opposed by Georgia's governor, Lester Maddox.

One remembers Maddox as the man who earned his first public reputation by chasing black men out of his restaurant with a pistol in one hand, an axe handle in the other. (He claimed later that the press had lied: "It was really a pick handle," Lester Maddox said.) The night before the fight, we are all conscious of where we are. It may be Atlanta, "the oasis of the South," but it is still very much the South.

"What do you think about the Governor's announcement declaring the day of your fight with Quarry a day of mourning?" a reporter asks.

"A day of what?" Ali answers.

"A day of mourning—m-o-u-r-n-i-n-g."

"I don't know what that means."

"You know, a sad day . . . . a *black* day."

"Oh, that! Yes, *that* we gonna have."

But Atlanta's young Jewish mayor, Sam Massell, has answered Maddox's statement. Aware that in addition to the Ali–Quarry fight, Atlanta is also having important pro and college football games as well as a pro basketball game, the Mayor makes *his* announcement: "Next week," he says, "will be Sport *Spectacular* week." It is the semifinal: Massell versus Maddox. Does Ali enjoy these white men and their sparring?

"No more popping off, no more boasting," Ali pronounces. "I don't want no more trouble. Just the fight with Quarry."

But, in fact, until this last evening before the fight, his public mood has not been happy; on the contrary, it has been sullen, it has been stern and almost frozen—a strange role for ebullient Ali. But in some ways he doesn't seem to be thinking of Quarry. In fact, Ali seems obsessed with a hard-punching black man named Joe Frazier. Watching him work, I am thinking about myself as well as him.

After all, Muhammad Ali is a complicated man and so am I. We both have gone through many of the same experiences. We both became World Champions. But Ali has aroused the minds of many people, mine included. I never did. Still, some of the experiences that made Ali a fighter made me a fighter. The details might be considerably different, but the ingredients are not. So, I'm watching him and thinking about him. I'm either better equipped or worse equipped to understand him than anybody else.

October 18, 1970: The week before the fight. We are in the Sports Arena, an old boxing gymnasium on the Southwest side of Atlanta, a mixed neighborhood.

Ali is sparring in the ring and looks fast. His legs get him out of trouble with the speed which has won him the label of "the fastest heavyweight of all time." His jab is coming fast and hard, perhaps even harder than before his exile. He is hitting with accuracy and concentrating on punching with more power. His combination punches carry speed and authority. His performance is consistent, his breathing, normal. Trainers Angelo Dundee and Drew "Bundini" Brown are both satisfied. But one thing seems to be worrying them: Ali's thinking. The trainers can't figure out what's on Ali's mind. And he's not doing much talking.

"I'm not predicting this time," he says from the ring after finishing eight rounds of boxing.

"Do you think you'll be able to *perform* in the fight as well as you look in the gym?" I ask Ali. (Fighters rate themselves on performance. If they were usually no good in school, now they score themselves 60%, 80%, 95%.)

"That's a good question," he says and he smiles. A long pause. "You are not as dumb as you look."

My imagination is taking me into a boxing ring with Ali. There I think my thoughts, while also trying to think his. I throw punches (questions). Ali counters them (answers). Then I react by faking that I was not hit (when, in fact, I was). Or else I pretend I'm punching harder (when, in fact, I'm not).

Of course, Muhammad Ali is aware that workouts in gymnasiums are one thing; actual fights another.

What is involved is a basic transition; in the gym a champion knows he's the superior man. The guy in front of him is being paid to get his employer in top condition.

Both fighters, the employer and the employee, wear big gloves and head guards. A round can be stopped at any time by the trainers in charge. The sparring partner, the employee, is not usually well-known; the employer is, in most cases, a champion or leading contender.

So, sparring partners have a special respect for champions. A champ has the psychological advantage. There are no pressures on the champ. The objective, impersonal, cold attitude a professional champion must have is, almost always, not used in the gym. A champ becomes unprofessional. He takes it easy with his sparring partner. Usually, a champ gets hit much more often in the gym than he does in the actual fight. (But not as hard.) In fights a champ uses every ingredient which supposedly has made him a champ. And one of the ingredients is fear. Fear is nonexistent in the gym. But in fights it comes to your rescue, or at least it does when you can control it.

Now, Ali's trainers and many of his supporters see in Ali a different man. Nobody can be certain he has the old, positive confidence which had made him a great fighter.

The training is over. Ali stares at the ceiling of the dressing room for minutes. It gets his people nervous.

"What are you thinking about?" one of them asks. There is no answer, and the trainer says: "Are you thinking about Quarry?"

"Quarry?" Ali answers ironically. "Who's he?" His eyes are still fixed on the ceiling. Ali is distracted by thoughts not connected with the fight. His body looks in great shape, but his mind seems off.

I'm looking at Ali. He's a new man—how much, I have to think, has he been affected and influenced by newspaper articles and by all the opinions of people other than Elijah Muhammad? That simple time when only one man knew the truth and that man was the Prophet of God and the leader of the Black Muslims is gone, that time is gone. There are worried looks on the faces of those close to Ali.

Of course, most of the sportswriters have picked Ali to win. As far as I'm concerned, they've done so for the wrong reasons. They go by how Ali looks in the gym, as opposed to how Quarry looks in the gym. Not me. I saw Quarry throwing a lot of leather. I saw him getting hit with shots by opponents who were faster than him. But I also saw Quarry pressing at all times. I saw him maintain a pressure which I didn't like a bit. Furthermore, I saw a fantastic enthusiasm in his attitude.

But the writers here only see when he gets hit, when he throws the "crazy" punches, when he begins to breathe hard after boxing two or three rounds. They are not aware of the pressure, they can't realize that Ali has been off for a long time, perhaps during his prime, and that consistent pressure by Quarry could produce the biggest upset in boxing history. If Ali's physical ability has been deteriorated by the three-and-a-half year absence, I still think he has enough confidence to overcome that factor. That's why I pick Ali to win. I pick him because I think that Ali has enough confidence and enough will to overcome whatever superior physical ability Quarry should have for all these years of fighting while Ali was inactive.

Naturally, many people are praying for a Quarry victory. Besides being the recognized number one contender, Quarry is white. He has become a sophisticated version of those old "White Hopes" they used to bring in against Jack Johnson when he was the first black heavyweight champion.

Three-and-a-half years of exile in his own land probably taught Ali more than Jack Johnson ever learned. With Elijah Muhammad to reinforce the rhetoric of his religion, he has grown up. In press conferences he is more subdued. He doesn't brag or laugh with the same intensity as when he was a young champion. Sometimes he jokes and makes newsmen laugh, but he always evades political or social subjects. Not once does he mention Black Muslims. Ali is not what he was during his preparations for the 1964 Championship fight againt Sonny Liston, when he had screamed, insulted and threatened his opponent. Nor is he the same Ali who, during the weigh-in ceremonies for that fight, was so out of control that doctors diagnosed him as "running scared."

October 26, 1970: George Plimpton spends the day in Ali's quarters in the suburban home of the man responsible for bringing the fight to Atlanta, Georgia, State Senator Leroy Johnson. "I was trying to talk to Ali and it was impossible," says Plimpton. "He was either on the phone, watching films, or busy with a lot of friends who went to him for fight tickets." I decide it is a good sign. It reminds me of the old unconventional Ali.

As the day moves into the hour for the fight, as in all of his previous fights, he does not "rest" enough.

Minutes before he is supposed to go to the Atlanta City Auditorium, he goes downtown and stands in front of the Regency-Hyatt, stage-managing bus accommodations for his army of followers, then waiting for the notoriously tardy Mrs. Martin Luther King, Jr. Having held the crowd for over thirty minutes, he finally gives up and steps into a car with Dundee, Bundini, Plimpton and a few close friends and leaves for the arena.

Walking toward the back entrance of the Auditorium, Ali can't evade the screaming crowd in the streets. He stops and shakes hands with a few and tells them to get in on time. "You better get there early," Ali yells, "You might be too late."

"What round?" the crowd wants to know. No answer.

Fogs of nicotine, and the crowd vibrating like a motor with small roars of expectation. The crowd, with the exception of hundreds of reporters from all over the world, is almost all black.

Up in the balcony are blacks from Atlanta and poor blacks who hitched in from other states. At ringside are the prosperous.

They are black and beautiful. Men in full-length ermine coats, mink hats, diamond pins and velvet, dressed as beautifully as the women. Everyone models his clothes for the crowd, the cameras and the press. In fact, those in the press aren't without their little vanities, too.

Autograph-seekers surround the black celebrities that only Ali could bring to his fights. Diana Ross sits near Ali's corner. Bill Cosby is in the front press row, commenting on the fight for closed-circuit TV and alternately clowning for the crowd. And spread around the first row behind the press in ringside seats are Sidney Poitier, Whitney Young, Julian Bond, The Supremes, Mrs. Martin Luther King, Jr., the Rev. Ralph Abernathy, Henry Aaron and Donn Clendenon among others. Everyone from the black ticket-takers to the black announcer (who later handed the microphone over to New York's Johnny Addie) makes this a "Black Day" indeed in Atlanta history.

The motif even carries over into the singing of the Star Spangled Banner, when rock singer Curtis Mayfield delivers the lyrics in the style of José Feliciano.

Beneath this brilliance of the surface, there is, however, a large lack of preparation. It is a complete reflection of the expectation that the fight would never happen, plus the unprofessionalism of many of those involved in putting it on. For Atlanta has not had a fight of any major proportions since 1939. No one in the city seems to have any idea of how to put this one on. The day before the fight I was laughing as I watched some of the executives of Sports Action, the promoters, working and sweating to help the carpenters finish the tiers of press seats. Just minutes before the preliminaries start, handlers are running all over ringside looking for nonexistent corner stools (which had to be purchased at the neighborhood hardware store after the prelims started and which still bore their price tags ($3.98) when brought into the ring). Even the gloves for the Ali–Quarry fight have been left at the airport! One of the fight promoters takes a cab to get them. What a sweat! Harold Conrad, the public relations man, is going crazy. He tries to organize. The man at the ticket door is having an argument with a local reporter. "I want my ticket right now," yells the reporter. "There is no ticket here for you," responds the man at the window. "Get Conrad," demands the reporter.

Now someone comes to Harold. "Mr. Conrad," the messenger says to the publicist. "A famous reporter is at the window without a ticket."

"Fuck him."

"But . . ."

"Fuck him," repeats Conrad and keeps walking.

Preliminary fights are over. Johnny Addie is now in the middle of the ring. He introduces the celebrities. Bill Cosby is called up. He goes into the ring and begins shadowboxing. Sidney Poitier jumps in and begins doing the same in the opposite corner. People now seem relaxed. Poitier and Cosby are killing time before closed-circuit TV goes on the air for the real show.

Now the ring empties. Only announcer Addie and referee Tony Perez, both from New York, are in the ring.

Suddenly there is a rush of sound. Heads turn toward the south side of the Auditorium. Coming is Jerry Quarry. He is moving nervously toward the ring with his trainer, Teddy Bentham, in front of him.

His face is shining from the grease his trainers have put on to protect him from cuts. Quarry seems to hold the hard, determined attitude he had displayed during his gym workouts. He is dressed in a robe that covers his blue trunks. Bentham is whispering something in his ear.

Last-minute instructions are always necessary. Not simply because the fighter is really listening to them, but because it gives a sort of psychological satisfaction. If there is a flaw that Quarry or Bentham has just discovered, it is too late to correct it.

They reach the ring and Bentham goes up first to get in between the second and the last rope so Quarry can get in without effort. All eyes are on Quarry, who is now throwing punches at an invisible opponent. He walks toward a neutral corner and begins rubbing his white and red striped boxing shoes over grains of resin, to prevent him from slipping.

Now the crowd stands up and begins to scream hysterically. Muhammad Ali is making his entrance. Ali has not heard this kind of noise for three-and-a-half years. He walks through the wild and screaming crowd, throwing punches at the air. Angelo Dundee is ahead of him while Bundini Brown follows from the rear. Atlanta's police surround them. The volume of the cheering increases as Ali steps into the ring and he acknowledges it by doing the "Ali shuffle," crisscrossing his legs like lightning and then coming up with a left jab. The screaming can be heard all over Atlanta.

Now both fighters are in the ring. In one corner Tony Perez waits for the announcer to introduce the fighters. After weeks of the wildest rumors of intervention by Maddox, the American Legion, the super patriots, the KKK and the Daughters of the Confederacy, nothing seems able to stop the fight now. For the first time since the announcement of the fight, there is the final confidence that there is a fight.

From the south side of the Auditorium, movie and television cameras move from one side of the ring to the other, focusing on the fighters. The fight is going to be seen in more countries than any other fight yet put on. Even Russia is interested in watching it.

Announcer Johnny Addie picks up the microphone. Ringside celebrities are introduced. Then, Addie introduces Quarry, who receives a good ovation. But, when the announcer tries to introduce Ali to the waiting crowd, they yell and scream so loudly no one hears his name. Ali is not introduced as a champion. But everyone there knows he is the real champion. Income from the fight is expected to be more than anything ever earned by Joe Frazier.

Referee Tony Perez signals both fighters to the middle of the ring for the traditional instructions. The audience is now quiet. Ali comes into the middle of the ring with trainers Angelo Dundee and Drew Bundini Brown. Quarry steps forward. Suddenly, we see Ali's lips moving—then Quarry's.

"You are in trouble, man. I'm going to get rid of you, fast," Ali says through his mouthpiece.

"Shut up and fight," is Quarry's answer. By now Perez is able to control the situation again. Ordering the fighters to remain quiet, the referee repeats the instructions.

The fighters begin to move to their respective corners and in the noise of the crowd, we head the sound of the bell. It is the first second of the first round of Ali's return.

CHAPTER 2

I'm nervous. My hands are tapping on my closed typewriter. My fingers are moving independent of my thoughts. Let me be honest. I want Ali to win.

Ali walks over to Quarry and throws in a hard left jab. Quarry moves back and shakes his head slowly from side to side as if saying no in disgust. It has hurt too much for a jab. Ali follows up with two . . . three fast jabs and a straight right cross behind the last jab. Each punch lands clean on Quarry's face. Surprisingly, Ali is on the offensive and he is driving Quarry backwards, who seems as shocked as me.

I'm trying to put my thoughts together, but a black man from New York, who is seated just behind me, in the first row behind the press, grabs me and begins to yell, "He's got him. He's got him."

Quarry throws his first punch, a wild left hook, that passes a foot from Ali's face and now another jab by Ali finds its target again. The crowd stands up. Ali is throwing punches, a flurry of punches and Quarry is bobbing and weaving. Ali is making the fight and he looks good doing it.

It's obvious. For the last two days I've been telling Ali that he had to show Quarry, early in the fight, who the boss was. That his past attitude of concentrating on defense in the first round while making his opponent look silly was not proper after being inactive for so long. Ali hadn't answered. In fact, he had turned me off, changing the subject. When Angelo Dundee would bring the matter back, Ali would completely ignore the conversation. But Angelo knew better. Ali would leave and think about it, digest the whole conversation and he would make the decision.

"Wise guy," I say, watching Ali doing just what I'd said.

Two minutes have passed in the first round and Ali is consistent with the attack. He is moving forward, chasing Quarry who is trying, unsuccessfully, to set himself. Strange. Quarry is known as one of the best counter-punchers in the game; undoubtedly the best counter-attacker among the heavyweights. But, I always knew Ali is not the best man to counter-punch. Ali is accurate with his punches and he has some of the best timing I've seen in boxing. He combines, almost to perfection, his accuracy and coordination with his speed.

But, included among the so many other "wrong" things that Ali does, he doesn't put body or full shoulder behind the punches. His punches are strictly from the arm, which should logically have no power. Automatically, Ali doesn't have to come close to his opponent to connect. He's always at a safe distance, which is to say that while Ali's timing is taking advantage of his own long reach, it's very difficult for an opponent to counter. Especially if that opponent is moving back—giving Ali not only the needed space for one of his many specialties, but also motivating Ali to do more of the same, while at the same time relaxing his mind to think of other tricks.

Quarry is encouraging Ali to look good, by doing the opposite. Quarry is moving away. Quarry is walking backward and he can't get set to take clean shots at Ali. Ali is in complete control.

I look at my watch. There are thirty seconds to go. Quarry throws another wild hook. It misses by six inches. Ali, still pressing, throws two and three jabs, then pushes Quarry back after missing the punches. Ten seconds to go and Ali misses a combination of six punches, not one of them hit the target. Quarry throws a right to the body and follows with a left hook to the head; the right is blocked by Ali's low hands, the hook misses by three inches.

At the bell, both fighters look at each other. Ali, satisfied for what he did. Quarry aware of what Ali couldn't do.

"Is that all you have to offer, motherfucker?" Quarry's Irish temper seems to say. "Let's see if you can take mine, motherfucker. You ain't nothing, motherfucker." It was the strongest word his face suggested—"motherfucker." And it seemed to suggest it all the time.

Ali has more class. He's the fighter who has learned his lies perfectly. "I was testing your devil's white face," his face says. "Now I'm going to play with you. I'm going to have fun with you." And he fakes a smile.

If I were Quarry, I would press Ali. I would use each and every ounce of my ability to force Ali back. After all, Ali's most comfortable style is to move, shooting punches while strolling backward. So I would do what I did against Willie Pastrano: "cut" the ring short. You don't follow a fast-moving target around. You short-cut him, worry him, try to disturb his thoughts, and his pattern will be destroyed. You don't follow him, you meet him. He moves backward and to his right; you simply move to your left first and then forward. If he goes farther backward and to his left, you simply move to your right and then in. His instinct would be to move backward again. But this time the ropes are gong to be there. You've cut the ring short.

I'm nervously trying to write something down in my pad. "Big round for Ali," I write down. But my mind tells me that my eyes saw something more. Ali came out in the first to establish that he was in command. He threw probably two hundred punches in the course of three minutes. In the first minute he connected ninety percent of the time; in the second minute, sixty-five percent; in the third, maybe twenty percent.

One of two things had happened—or both. Ali's inability to hurt Quarry had taken the confidence out of the punches, or Quarry, who seemed paralyzed the first thirty seconds of the fight, was losing respect for Ali's power and was, in the last part of the first round, getting confident himself.

I'm surprised by the sound of the bell for the second round. The one-minute rest went fast. I'm trembling now. Ali comes out with care. He seems to be pacing himself. "I did too much in the first," I'm thinking, as if Ali is actually saying it. Ali throws a slow jab. Quarry bends and from there shoots a roundhouse jumping left hook that barely misses Ali. Ali steps back and jabs again. He's more careful now and for the first time I see worry in his face. "Three-and-a-half years layoff," he's thinking. Three-and-a-half years of getting his fighting heart soft, sensible and rational; three-and-a-half years of seeing and being conscious of the hungry blacks and talking with white students who agreed with him; three-and-a-half years exercising all those intellectual muscles which are not necessarily used in fights (before, during or after). So Muhammad Ali is now suffering the misery of having his mental and physical boxing muscles out of condition. He's carrying the inertia of three-and-a-half years of not throwing punches on those days he was ready to.

"Do this," his mind says and the body responds in the affirmative. "Do that," and the body again obeys. It is not a betrayal. It is not the clash of the wrong messages making the body react poorly or the right messages with the body unable to respond properly. The body is doing what the mind is telling it to do. The combination is perfect; perfect in its imperfection. What happens with the mind is that parts of it have been overworked; parts of it are out of condition, untrained, influenced, distracted. Ali's brain is reacting to what it sees. But Ali's brain is not seeing everything.

So, it's up to Quarry to see what I'm seeing. And he's not that dumb.

But, is it possible? Can Quarry "see" what I see? Let's see.

He's putting on the pressure now. Ali is backing off. A hook and a straight right both make contact with Ali's stationary head. "What's happening to Ali?" the man from New York asks me. But I can't talk. "Move," I yell. "Side-to-side, Ali."

Quarry has just found his formula. The pressure is on. It's going to be a long night for Ali. Two hooks by Quarry. Both are blocked by Ali. Forty seconds remaining in the second round, and the fight seems to be turning. Ali misses a jab. Misses another. Quarry is now able to counter. He is closer to Ali. Now Ali is going back toward the ropes. Quarry follows. Quarry's first effective punch, a powerful left hook to Ali's body, lands. Ali's right elbow drops automatically. It is a reaction. Now Quarry is punching Ali with fury and Ali is lying against the ropes.

Why? I ask myself. Just three days ago, Ali told me in private that the only reason why Joe Frazier looked so good in fights is because his opponents always lay back on the ropes, giving Frazier room to unleash his attack. "That's why Frazier looks good," Ali told me. "Once you give him a stationary target, he becomes the bravest Nigger in America." Adding, "Only a fool or a dope would do that."

Well, he was doing it now. Of course, the conversation had aroused him because I had criticized him for doing in the gym—lying back against the ropes—what he is doing in the ring now. "Well, over here I simply test different things," he had said. I had believed him.

Now he was at a competitive level still doing what he did in the gymnasium. He can't do otherwise. He can't help doing what he's doing. He fell into a habit. Can't fight any longer. His mind is off. My thoughts are clear. I look across the ring and I see Cus D'Amato, my former manager. He had also managed former heavyweight king, Floyd Patterson. We knew each other pretty well. In fact, we had very few disagreements. Our eyes met. Our thoughts were the same. I knew he was worried. He knew I was worried.

The bell relieves me a little. And, as he walks back to his corner, Bundini Brown throws water in Ali's face. Dundee starts to give instructions. The crowd is enjoying the fight. The man from New York asks me, "What's going on with my man here? He's changed."

"He's just fucking around," I lie. "He'll be O.K."

Some of the few boxing writers who have some understanding about fighting exchange looks. Jimmy Cannon asks, with a gesture, the same thing the man from New York has asked me. "Don't worry," I gesture back.

Just yesterday Quarry had told me: "I'm not going into the ring with the idea that Clay's three-and-a-half year layoff is going to affect his stamina." Then, with an unconscious half-smile as if hoping to be wrong, he said: "He might be in better shape now than he was four years ago."

I thought I heard two bells for the commencement of the third round.

I'm completely shook up. Ali comes out slowly from his corner. Quarry seems more alert. Ali attempts to pull his head away from a feint and Quarry connects a straight right to Ali's body. Ali counters with a light left hook and a sloppy right; both punches bounce off Quarry's gloves.

Ali begins to feint now. He is trying to get Quarry to lead. Quarry walks toward Ali. A left is short by an inch, a right con-

nects and Ali steps back. Not hurt, just frustrated. For a thinking man like Ali, reasons can be found for pain. But frustration
stands close to defeat. Doubt at any given moment is acceptable.
But frustration? That's the devil penetrating an athlete.

Frustration is the enemy. The worst of them. Let me explain.
Frustration closes a switch in your brain. Your concentration is
lost. It is because you begin to search more and more frantically
for the cause or causes that create your frustration. If you find
them, then of course it ceases to be frustration. It is your inability to find the causes that create the panic. So a real pro like Ali
looks for an alternative.

The only real alternative to continued frustration is guts, heart,
balls—"cojones"—which means, "I'm not going to quit. I won't
make it easy for him." The will to win begins to disappear; the
balls to stay on your two feet remains.

Another Quarry left hook finds its target. Ali moves back and
Quarry follows with confidence. Ali stops Quarry with a stiff left
jab. Ali follows with a right that glances off Quarry's head. Now
they get inside. There is a short exchange. Quarry steps back. He
rubs his left glove over his left eye. Ali *runs* towards Quarry. And
Quarry now has his back against me. Ali's connecting.

Blacks are standing up and screaming at the ring. Ali now
seems in control. A jab hits Quarry hard, his head is pushed back.
Ali repeats the jab, follows with a straight right-left hook—right
uppercut—left hook—right hand, ra-tat-tat-tat-tat-tat. The
punches are being thrown to predetermined areas.

Quarry is forced to concentrate on defense. His face now is
toward me. Ali is throwing fast combinations to the head of
Quarry. Blood covers Quarry's face and chest. He seems to be
badly cut. "You were right," said the man from New York and
he is excitedly grabbing my jacket.

Ali is a tiger. His attitude resembles that of Quarry's in the
previous round. There is the bell.

Quarry is protesting the cut. He's kicking the floor. Teddy Bentham pushes Quarry down and begins to work on the cut. Teddy is one of the best cut men in the business. Teddy is a cool, undramatic man who is not bothered too easily. But now his white hair seems to stand up on his head. His glasses are spotted with blood. It's not the Teddy Bentham I know. "The fight is over," I tell the man from New York.

As the man from New York begins to disagree with me, the bell sounds. Quarry pushes Bentham to the side. Referee Tony Perez is called by Bentham. There's an argument between Quarry, his trainer and Perez. Perez makes an about-face and crisscrosses both arms vigorously. The fight is over. Ali opens his arms. Bundini embraces Ali. Quarry, tears rolling down his cheeks, charges Ali. Bentham steps between them. "Why? Why?" Quarry seems to be asking.

If a Black Muslim has any doubt about Allah, this is the time to believe. Allah is with Ali tonight.

Blacks scream. Strangers embrace. "He's great, isn't he?" the man from New York asks of no one in particular.

I look across the ring and see that Cus D'Amato is there talking with someone. I'm not satisfied with Ali's work. I think he was in trouble and the cut saved him.

Cops and Black Muslims are walking Ali to his dressing room. People are pushing themselves in to take a close glimpse of Ali, who is smiling.

Quarry is not getting the same attention. He's a loser. People don't like losers.

I talk to Cus now. We ask each other the same question. What's happening to Ali? Not many fighters are happy to see their ex-managers. Usually, they bring sad thoughts. For fighters blame managers, with justice, as the cause of their bad economic condition.

But Cus D'Amato is a hell of a man. I've met a lot of people in boxing. None have the knowledge of Cus. He has a few scattered white hairs on his head but they do not hide those shining muscles on his scalp which move as he talks. He talks and one is compelled to listen. Even those who hate him have to listen to him. Boxing is always his subject. But people who did not know who he was, would never think of Cus as a fight manager. He speaks too well. And because he is sincere about boxing, he offers continuing challenge to the men who control it. The boxing establishment doesn't like Cus; they hate him.

His philosophy of boxing is simple. "Boxing," he says, "is an absolutely reasonable activity." By this measure, Ali was not too reasonable.

"Ali is not a good fighter," Cus says. "He's the luckiest boxer around. He would have never won this fight if Quarry had not been cut. He was in trouble. I know and *you* know. Cus now adds, "He is a deteriorating fighter. His mind needs work."

People have told me that in his childhood Cus thought of becoming a priest. Now he is really boxing's unfrocked high priest. He's the inventor of the peek-a-boo style. He teaches his fighters to carry their hands high, close to the cheeks and to punch from that defensive position. He tries to create a perfect machine. And when the machine starts working, the real training begins. Cus starts to train his fighter's head. He has long conversations with his fighters and Cus brings out into words what every fighter feels but can't explain. "In professional boxing when you step into the ring you will come to understand that you are there to participate in a contest of wills, not of abilities." (Of course, he is assuming the abilities are roughly equal.)

Now this man is in front of me saying that Ali is not a good fighter. "Ali is aware that he is slower," Cus says. "He has lost confidence in his speed. As a result he *is* slower and, as you could see, he performed like an ordinary fighter. In the past, he could get away with a lot of mistakes, because of his fantastic speed. Now he's losing that and he is going to find out that he is not *that* smart in the ring. He doesn't have *any* alternative for his speed. He is losing his best asset."

Cus is saying that Ali's habit of pulling away from punches, exposing his jaw with his hands low, is a fatal mistake. It doesn't allow him to fight inside. Furthermore, his punches have no power because Ali thrusts out punches with his arms, without the heavier foundation of the shoulders and body. After finishing a punch or punches, Ali moves away by walking backward instead of moving to the sides or ducking, which the "book" would call for. "If you're standing on a railroad track and the train comes, you can't move backward. You either lay down on the floor or step to the side," Cus says.

I remember that Cus had worked on a documentary film about Ali five weeks ago and had sparred with Ali for a few seconds.

"Tell me, Cus," I say. "Tell me about your sparring with Muhammad." Cus now smiles. He pushes me down into a chair and starts to whisper.

"He was showing off with his 'Ali shuffle,' " Cus says. "telling me he was so fast with his invention that nobody could touch him. I laughed and he said to me, 'That's right, old man, nobody can touch me!' I say: 'Mr. Ali, one doesn't have to be a fighter to prove you wrong!' Well, he didn't like that. 'What can *you* do?' Ali said. So we stood up facing each other and Ali did the Ali shuffle, crisscrossing his feet with great speed. Stopped and threw a jab. And I simply did this . . ." Cus took up a boxer's stance, then bent his body quickly to the right and extended his left hand straight out, in the direction of my stomach.

" 'You caught me by surprise,' Ali said to me," continued Cus. "And I said: 'That's what one is supposed to do.' Ali got really mad," Cus insists. "He got so mad that he wanted to do it again. And I knew he wanted to do it again to trick me." Cus sat down and pushed by a mysterious spring got up again.

"You see," he says with a broad smile on his face, "he knew I had outsmarted him the first time and he wanted to get even. And I knew what he was going to do. What was going on in his head." Cus again assumes the position from which he had surprised Ali. "You see that," he says, showing me his whole left side exposed. "That's exactly what he saw when I had tricked him, but he had seen it too late.

"Well," Cus sustains the pace, "I pretended that I didn't want to fool around. But Ali insisted and I made him 'force' me to do it again." Cus now looks around to make sure no one is listening. Some of the crowd is still waiting for Ali to come out of his dressing room. "Just as I had expected, when he stopped the Shuffle, I bent exactly as before, and when he made his move to punch with a right to my left side, I came up with my right, beating him to the punch and right here," Cus touches the left side of my jaw. "Right here.

"I drew blood from his mouth. 'He cut me, he cut me,' Ali yelled, spitting a little blood. 'Man, you are fast,' he said to me. But how can I be fast. A man 60 years old can't be fast. It is . . ."

"Timing," I interjected.

"Well," Cus says with pride like a teacher proud of his favored student, "you know what I'm talking about. You see, you know!"

Once again there was no disagreement between Cus and me. Now we both walk toward the post-fight press conference where both fighters—first Quarry, then Ali—were expected to talk to the press.

I try to get into Ali's dressing room and for the second time an Atlanta cop stops me. "If you don't have a pink ticket," the cop says, "you can't get in." I show him a blue ticket. "A pink one," the big, rough-looking, white cop says, his voice sounds uncomfortable as it saying, "I've been forced to work for a nigger and no nigger is going to fuck over me."

Ali is coming out. I see Angelo and Bundini with him, also Ferdie Pacheco, Ali's private physician, and a group of Black Muslims. They know me. So, I walk toward Ali. "I want to talk to you later," I whisper into Ali's ear. He keeps walking, thinking for ten seconds and grabs my left ear. "Room 1808, Regency."

Cops and Black Muslims keep the small crowd away from Ali. "Go there," Ali says to me and repeats: "1808 . . . Lots of 'foxes.' Go." Now he disappears into the crowd to face newsmen. He looks not that happy. Post-fight conferences bore him. He is going to face men, many of whom will hit Ali harder than Quarry did. Because nothing hurts more than answering dumb questions with a straight face. These questions are usually asked by tired men who satisfy themselves asking stupid questions to "stupid men"—fighters.

I never took press conferences seriously. I played dumb to the press. And when I would slip and answer a question unlike let's say, "Hurricane" Jackson or Frankie DePaula, they would say, "This is a special fighter. He knows what he's talking about." And they, the press, made Patterson, Ali and myself and a few others, exceptions among fighters. Ones who could answer questions.

"I hate this shit," I tell Cus, referring to the press conference. "I'm going to the hotel. I'll see you later." Outside some people wait for Ali to come out.

It's past twelve and I'm still thinking about the fight. I'm supposed to write a story for the *San Juan Star*, the only English language daily in Puerto Rico, but I want to wait for personal interviews with Quarry and Ali. I always felt that it was better to "interview" fighters fighter-to-fighter fashion, rather than sounding like a boxing writer. Then we could use the same language—we could read between the lines. Fighters lie to one another with class. This is the story of our lives. We lie. If we don't lie in the ring, then we get hit.

So I'm thinking hard and my imagination takes me to the Regency-Hyatt House where I'm talking with Ali. No one else is there. I have the interview in advance in my head. "Tell me about the fight," I will ask. And Ali won't even hesitate. "Just like I planned," he will say. "Showed him I was boss in the first; gave a little confidence to the poor man in the second; and decided to finish him off in the third."

"You are talking to me, man," I will say.

"You saw what I did to the bum. It was no contest."

"Wasn't it?"

"Well," he will say with big and false logical persuasion, "ask the judges and the referee. They'll bear me out."

Champions and good fighters are champions and good fighters because they can lie better than the others. The first thing you learn in the gym is that you have to have a double personality if you are to become a good fighter. Basically, you must have the discipline to lie when you're hitting the heavy bag, the speed bag, or human flesh. Then, when you come out of the gym your lies should be deposited in a very special corner of your brain.

Because we fighters understand lies. What's a feint? What's a left hook off the jab? What's an opening? What's thinking one thing and doing another? What's getting tired?

A feint is an outright lie. You *make believe* you're going to hit your opponent in one place, he covers the spot and your punch lands on the other side. A left hook off the jab is a classy lie.

You're converting an I into an L. Making openings is starting a conversation with a guy, so another guy (your other hand) can come and hit him with a baseball bat.

I was an expert about thinking one thing and making my body do something else. I had a special apparatus which we called "Willie," consisting of a mattress wrapped around a post. We would draw a human figure on it. Then we would put numbers in the vulnerable spots (jaw, ribs, solar plexus, stomach). My manager, D'Amato, would sit near me and call numbers. I would throw the punch. There was a time when I threw six punches to predetermined areas in two-fifths of a second. Nobody believed it. Believe me! It sounded like one big punch.

The point I'm trying to make is that there were times when Cus would call say, 7–2–1–4–1–2 (left jab, straight right, left hook, right uppercut, left hook, right cross) and my mind would digest the numbers, send the message to my body, and my body would throw, 7–2–5 (left to the body)–1–2–1. A different combination. I would even double-cross Cus.

Enter Muhammad Ali. These lies are the description of Ali. He is not a good fighter, so says D'Amato, much less a great fighter. But he is the champion of the world. Which, believing Cus, and I do, makes Ali a genius. (Because only a genius could prove Cus wrong.)

Ali is not a great fighter in the conventional sense that Sugar Ray Robinson, Willie Pep and Joe Louis were. Each of these fighters knew every punch and every move and added some tricks to the book, that unwritten book whose teachings are passed on from gym to gym and are the nearest thing we have to our own culture.

Robinson was the master. He moved well, had tremendous power in both hands, punched in combinations and very seldom made mistakes inside the ring.

Joe Louis used his fantastic speed of hands as his defensive weapons; he punched continuously and had one of the best jabs in the business. He didn't punch in flurries, he punched in combination. Six punches in combination with each of them powerful enough to shake a building.

Pep was the boxer. He invented moves that fighters began using after him. Pep, like Ali, was not known as having the punching power of a giant mechanical hammer, he simply punched often enough and hard enough to be considered a great fighter.

Muhammad Ali, unlike Robinson, doesn't have the power Robinson had. Unlike Louis, Ali doesn't use his punching for defense and he doesn't move like Pep. Nevertheless, Ali is the superior fighter of his time. We have a man who does not have the physical greatness of the greatest men of other times, yet no professional fighter has been able to beat him. And his fights remind us that Robinson, Louis and Pep used to get hit with many more punches in one fight than Ali received in twenty fights. The explanation is simple.

Muhammad Ali is a genius. He has a power that great fighters never had. Don't watch Ali's gloves, arms or legs when he's fighting. Watch his brains.

For when Muhammad Ali was Cassius Clay and was only twelve, his mental machine was already working. He was already independent enough to carry his hands low when told not to and smart enough to concentrate his interest on boxing.

His lies began. It was not that he wasn't listening to what people tried to teach him; it was that he interpreted teaching in his own way.

I imagine young Cassius Clay beginning to box with boys who were his equal. When hit, for carrying his hands low, Clay would move and move more, until he wasn't that easy to hit. Like me, when I began my own career, Clay found out that not getting hit was the most important quality for a fighter to learn. And defense is a matter of instincts. It is not that you are not supposed to get hit. It is the fact that *you know* you are not going to get hurt.

When you *really* know that you are not going to get hit, then two very important intellectual muscles are being exercised; the sense of anticipation and confidence. Not getting hit improves one's own desire; confidence builds up the will; desire, confidence and will feed your intelligence: the ability to think fast and the right mind-body coordination.

These are qualities that the naked eye can see. To hit an opponent without getting hit is another quality for the naked eye. But the forces which impel the strength and speed behind every one of a fighter's moves are invisible. This is for each individual fighter to see, to feel.

Now, after the Quarry fight, how could I judge Ali? He still had speed, but he made all those mistakes that make Cus D'Amato ill. Yet, once again, he had gotten away with them. Ali, in fact, had used his mistakes to fool the other guy. I thought I knew why. Ali knows when he's doing wrong. He invites you to take advantage of it. But Ali is two steps ahead. He *knows* what your next two punches are going to be.

I think a lot about Ali. I'm puzzled by him. This genius of a man violates every rule there is in the making of a good fighter and gets away with it. What could have happened if Ali had signed with D'Amato that long time ago when Ali was Clay and he, his father and his brother went to see Cus to see if he was interested in the young, upcoming Clay.

D'Amato was too busy in Indianapolis with his fighter, heavyweight champion, Floyd Patterson, then and couldn't really talk with Clay. But what would have happened if they (D'Amato and Clay) had gotten together?

Knowing Cus like my left hand and knowing Ali good enough to make a fairly good judgment about his behavior and his boxing career, I would say that it would have been a catastrophe. It would have been the clash of two opposite characters. Cus, imposing, strong, loyal to his boxing conviction and a do-as-I-say-or-else teacher. Ali, independent, strong, loyal to his instincts, and an I-do-what-I-want fighter. No match. For the good of both. Taking into account Clay's eventual ties with Black Muslims, it would have been a situation in which Cus would have had to go to the Mosque with Ali, and that's an impossibility.

But in my effort to understand the complexities of Muhammad Ali, I find myself disagreeing with Cus. Ali goes beyond what Cus can teach.

Ali doesn't have the physical tools of a great fighter. Ali doesn't punch with the power of Louis, Liston, Marciano, Walcott, Charles or even Floyd Patterson, who was small for a heavyweight champion. Ali doesn't seem to have the courage of Liston (at his greatest against Cleveland Williams) and Marciano; the killer instinct of Louis; the swiftness of Walcott; the speed of hands of Floyd. And Muhammad Ali doesn't punch to the body!

Remember when Max Schmelling fought Louis for the heavyweight crown in Yankee Stadium? The German had K.O.'d Louis a couple years before this fight and this time the German walked in confidently in the first round. Louis gave Schmelling such a bad beating in the first two minutes of fighting, knocking him down twice, that Schmelling's second had no choice but to jump into the ring to prevent his man from being actually crippled. It was body punches that did the trick. After the fight Schmelling had three broken ribs and never fought again.

Patterson softened Archie Moore in the body with murderous left hooks to the sides. Gasping for air, Moore walked into Floyd's famous leaping left hook, with glove (Floyd's) and chin (Moore's) making final contact and ending the match.

Marciano, Walcott and Charles all punched to the body. Muhammad Ali doesn't.

Of course, Walcott used to evade punches by stepping back with his legs or moving to the sides, then letting go particularly sneaky punches. His most outstanding quality was to trick his opponent. What a liar!

Louis' jab used to murder his opponent's will. It had the power of a right cross. Patterson's bob and weave was ideal to study. I saw him at the beginning of his reign as champion, and this man was—in my book—one of the best fighters I've ever seen. Patterson was the master, among the heavyweights, in throwing combination punches; a series of punches—two or more—to predetermined areas. I saw Floyd start a five-punch combination with an opponent, in which the first blow knocked the guy out, but too late to stop the combination. Floyd hit his descending rival with the remaining four punches.

Marciano was a tank. He entered the ring with strange ideas in his head: to trade punches, to test who had more power, who could take more pain, who was the man's man. But he had one thing: he was smart. He looked crude, with no class at all, and awkward. But watch his films today. Each of the men he beat, he did so by tricking them. He was also a good liar.

You compare these champions with Muhammad Ali and you come to a quick conclusion: Ali can't fight. Because Ali does exactly the opposite of what these past champions did. Ali doesn't step back like Walcott; doesn't bob and weave or have the combination punching power of Patterson; and he's certainly not interested in Marciano's philosophy of exchanging blows with another man.

And yet, I can't see any of these fighters beating him at his best with the exception of Floyd Patterson, on the night he knocked out Moore, or perhaps the way he looked his last few fights before becoming champion. For Floyd had the speed then to destroy Ali's assets.

But the genius in Ali takes his limitations and makes them virtues. Let us go step by step. I can't think of a past heavyweight champion whose punching power wasn't superior to Ali's. Yet in his first twenty fights, Ali, then Cassius Clay, won every one of them, scoring seventeen knockouts. The man who can't punch had a slugging average of .850, on the day he announced his alliance to the Black Muslims, the day after winning the heavyweight crown from "killer" Sonny Liston. Now, as Muhammad Ali, his average has dropped to .777. For a non-puncher, this average is still one of the very best. So what is Ali's mystery? Why does a man who every expert agrees has no punching power knock most of his opponents out, including a one-punch K.O. over Sonny Liston on Ali's first defense of his title?

The answer is in speed and timing. Clay then, and Ali now, has the ability to let punches go with extreme quickness, but most important, at the right moment, just before the man in front of him is able to put his boxer's sense of anticipation to work.

When that happens, the man getting hit doesn't see the punch. As a result, this man's brain can't prepare him to receive the impact of the blow. The eyes couldn't send the message back to the part of the body which would take the shock. So we arrive at one knockout of a conclusion: the punch that puts you to sleep is not so much the hard punch as the punch that you don't see coming.

But the knockout process is more complicated than that. It's a matter of will. A knockout could very well come at a time when a fighter is too proud to give up, but in a state of discouragement, "knowing" he can't acquire victory. His subconscious mind comes to his rescue. The fighter has a choice of two things: to get knocked out or to get tired and look awful in the ring. Some, those with iron balls, might *get tired* and finish the fight defeated and in a state of exhaustion. Others, not-so-tough, let themselves be separated from their senses.

Have you ever heard the story about the boxers who, after being "out on their feet, tired and beaten," get their second wind and come back to pull out the fight? The boxing writers who have created this myth should not be criticized for giving out misinformation. Boxing tends to deceive people. These second wind situations occur only when there are accidents. Like a fighter is tired and suddenly throws a punch which by luck hits the other man on the chin. The "tired" fighter becomes "untired," he becomes a tiger; he gets that famous "second wind." Many times he knocks his opponent out.

But in reality, the "tired" man had not run out of gas. The man *thought* he was tired. It was an excuse provided by the subconscious. If you don't believe me, take a car and let it run out of gas. Like D'Amato says, "You can kick it, curse it, threaten it, kiss it. The car won't move." The same is expected of a human being. One is either truly tired or is not. Most of the time, in the case of professional fighters, the ones who have trained properly, tiredness is purely psychological.

Muhammad Ali *knows* this. He has the power, conscious or instinctive, to tire out other fighters. For example, when Ali pulls away from a punch, which is wrong; when he carries his hands low, which is wrong; when he only punches to the head, which is wrong; the man's curious power is at work. And he wears out his opponents. Because doing these wrong things, he hits his opponents more often, while getting hit in return at an unbelievable minimum. He gives them frustration.

There he is with his hands down. It is an invitation to get his rivals to throw punches. But when he pulls away with his chin way up in the air in a provocative position, there is only one way to get that chin and that is getting close to Ali's anxious, quick hands. Usually, with his close-to-perfect timing, Ali can produce an impact between the forward movement of his right and the incoming movement of his opponent's chin. The encounter is often fatal for the man whose chin is rushing to meet the right-cross.

One other simple quality in Ali which undercuts D'Amato's theory is that my manager's philosophy is based entirely on a belief in reason. And I thought a lot about this in relation to Ali. I was very interested in the study of Ali's actions because there was a time when we were both champions and the possibility of a match between the two of us was near.

It seemed reasonable for me, if I fought him to work on Ali's body. It was Ali's waist which moved his head back, therefore, I, for one, would have to hit him in the body, knowing that his upper torso was too far back for his hands to come back in time for a counter. In other words, I would have worked at a distance where I could hit him in the body without being worried about him getting back at me in time, given my speed.

But again, what seems so obvious and reasonable to me should also have been reasonable to the others who had already met him. And believe me, Ali fought the best heavyweights of his time. Real pros. So here is when D'Amato's philosophy and Ali's artistic behavior clash. What happened to these men who could work over other fighters to the body but seem incapacitated by Ali, thus becoming unprofessional?

It could be that Ali's pre-fight antics—let us now call them maneuvers—hit the center nerve of these fighters' emotions. Ali's ability to bring out the uncontrollable emotions of his opposition could have been so enigmatically powerful, so insulting, so primitively inflammable, that in a very deep sense he made them street fighters again who had to try to "kill" him by connecting with his seldom-touched face. He must have created an anger which made one feel like breaking his jaw in different places at the same time. Wouldn't it be something if the uncanny Ali is not only unconsciously, but consciously, aware of this. What a genius!

Last night, of course, the fight ended on cuts. Perhaps Quarry got cut chasing the seemingly vulnerable chin. Perhaps (as in 95% of all cuts in boxing) the large gash was an accidental meeting of Ali's head and Quarry's face. The fact remains that the ghost of inconclusiveness is haunting D'Amato, Ali and my self. The fight ended too early and no one could really see if Ali still has those curious powers.

Well, these questions stayed in my head for the next few weeks, and you may be certain I was fascinated with the choice of Bonavena for his next opponent. Bonavena, the indestructible Bonavena, who had a chin as hard as a horseshoe!

CHAPTER 3

Oscar Bonavena is big and tough and has two words of English. They are "motherfucker" and "cocksucker." He is a white Argentinean and he is so strong he would probably argue that power is the only ingredient necessary to make good prize-fighters. While not as big and powerful as that other Argentinean, Luis Angel Firpo, el Toro de las Pampas, who once hit Jack Dempsey so hard that Dempsey landed in a sportswriter's lap, Bonavena is still a good puncher, who can always take a man out with one of his wild cannonball shots.

Two things these two paisanos had in common: they were both tremendously powerful with over-developed physiques and both possessed brains suitable for weightlifters. Their action in the ring depended entirely upon their physical mechanism. Whether training or in competition their brains lacked for use. That important muscle was always out of shape. But Bonavena had one thing that Firpo never had: balls. Bonavena was not an easy man to put down. Bonavena would put anybody into the most grueling test of them all: the test of wills.

Naturally, I felt Ali shouldn't be put into this kind of test so soon after Quarry. After all, Ali had gone only a total of three rounds in forty-three months, forty-three months of doing everything but boxing; for forty-three months Ali's mind had been diverted. As a matter of fact, his restlessness seemed to be caused as much by what he wanted for blacks in America as for what he wanted of his own boxing career. Consequently, for all that time, Ali learned more about other problems, about the real problems confronting the Muslims of his country. His boxing thoughts; his fistic concentration was distracted.

Given his performance against Quarry, it would have been more logical, I thought, to match Ali with an older fighter like Floyd Patterson who probably couldn't offer any serious danger to Ali any more, or even a rematch with George Chuvalo who might sweat out some of Ali's present weaknesses without the risk (in my opinion) of a Chuvalo victory. But not Bonavena. Bonavena scared me.

I had boxed Bonavena a few years back in the gym. I knew a little about him, and his attitude inside the ring. And if what I knew was correct, Ali was in trouble. Let me analyze Bonavena a little.

You can hit Bonavena and it's like giving food to a hungry man or electricity to a bulb. A punch to any part of Bonavena's body generates his desire to go on charging, punching, and asking for more, and that is, believe me, discouraging. This mule of a man violates in his own peculiar way, the basic of boxing. He doesn't follow at all the "I-hit-you-you-don't-hit-me" rationale. His philosophy seems to be, "You hit me and I hit you. Let's see who falls first."

The trouble with Bonavena is that getting hit doesn't concern him at all, to the contrary it appears as if your punches give him energy. So his theory is more: "Hit me and you generate my power, then I give *you* pain."

When I was in the ring with Bonavena, he assured me that he wasn't going to hurt me. "I'm much heavier," he had said, "and I know I shouldn't use my power on you."

"Use it," I remember answering, "but if you see that I'm hurt, then lay off." My ego began working. "If I hurt you," I continued, "I'll do the same."

After three rough rounds in which we went at each other with more than we normally thought to use in the gym, the other boxers stopped their workout to watch this Torres–Bonavena war and gave us a tremendous applause at the end.

"I didn't hurt you, did I?" Oscar asked me.

"No, you didn't," I said. "Did I hurt you?"

He smiled. "You are not a bad fighter," he said. Puerto Rican kids in the gym came up to me to whisper what a beating I had given the Argentinean heavyweight. Of course it was not a beating. I hit him plenty in the body. Bonavena missed every left hook or straight right he used to my head. A couple of times if he had hit me with one of them, he would have killed me. I was really watching for his big weapons.

I had a lot of confidence in myself then and I thought that a Torres-Ali fight would be a most interesting fight. I thought I had a formula to beat Ali. But being honest with myself I knew it would not be easy. Now, years later, that Torres-Ali fight out of my mind, and me retired, I still thought that Bonavena was nonetheless too dangerous for Ali, and this even though I once thought I could have beaten Bonavena. A question of style. A question of soul. Because Bonavena had a hell of a big soul. You never knew if he was an angel or a devil. I didn't think of most fighters that way, I tried to keep them where they were—problems for me to solve. But Bonavena was the real stuff you could not give a name to.

For style is another of the intricacies of boxing. I always knew it, but I learned it again the hard way. A Cuban named Florentino Fernandez once won over me by a technical knockout in the fifth. In turn, I beat my countryman José González. Yet González came back to knock out Fernandez. Yes, a question of style.

Besides—for Ali—Bonavena had an unhappy style. Besides being indestructible, Bonavena had a habit of throwing punches from every angle. He was a tropical storm that took unpredictable directions. Yes, I thought, no one knows where the next punch is going to come from. If you want to know how much will and heart your fighter has, and don't care too much about his looks, then match him against Bonavena.

But if you have doubt about your fighter's confidence and you love him, you don't put him in with Oscar. For Bonavena is a fighter who can't be discouraged or intimidated, nor can his will be destroyed. If you hit a man with your best shot, and he doesn't flinch, the thing to do is to keep hitting him until he falls. You have to keep doing it until the last second of the last round. Even if he still is not flinching, you might still have won the fight. But usually, when a man is hitting another man hard and continuously and the other man simply smiles and keeps coming at him, the man throwing the punches suffers. He can get discouraged, his will easily can leave him. And you have a loser. Besides, the ability to take punches as if he were a heavy bag and come bouncing back, is not the only thing Bonavena has. Bonavena also throws a lot of leather in those unexpected punches.

He punches hard. Very hard. I can refer to Joe Frazier. They had two encounters. In the first, On September 21, 1966, ten rounds, Bonavena dropped Frazier with a left hook in the fourth round. When the count reached eight and the referee waved them together, Bonavena hit him again, this time a straight right. Frazier went to the canvas again.

Two different punches had connected on Frazier's chin, each hard enough to send him to the canvas. Of course, he got up both times—he, too, had a will of iron—and, in fact, at the end of an unyielding, unruly, brutal fight, Frazier outpointed Bonavena. It had been close. Luckily for Frazier the fight was held in New York where scoring is by rounds. The two knockdowns only cost Frazier the loss of the round in which they occurred.

In California the story could have been reversed, for California scoring is by points and such a fight could, conceivably, have gone to Bonavena.

When they fought the second time, twenty-seven months later, Frazier had already won a version of the world's heavyweight crown. Pennsylvania was one of the few states in America which recognized Frazier as a champ. So, Philadelphia, the champ's hometown, became the site for his second defense of the title. The first had been against another Spanish fighter, Mexico's Manuel Ramos, who hadn't been able to take Frazier's savage attack past the second round.

The fight began with Frazier putting on his ever-present pressure. For ten rounds it looked as if Bonavena was going to be knocked out. But from the eleventh round on, Bonavena came back, became the dominant presence and made the fight. For the first time in all those rounds Frazier concentrated on defense. It had been the first time since the night he knocked out Buster Mathis in eleven rounds—for the world championship of New York, Pennsylvania and Massachusetts—that Frazier had gone over ten rounds.

So, for the second time, Bonavena threatened to beat Frazier. Yet, again at the end, with Frazier at the point of exhaustion, Bonavena had lost. His only consolation was that he had been the first to go the distance with Joe and had done it again, almost won again, not a poor showing when you consider that Frazier had a record of nineteen K.O.'s in twenty-two fights.

So it was likely that while Bonavena's unique style was hardly the kind of tune-up Ali needed, Bonavena had been the man who had given Frazier the most trouble. Ali and Dundee were probably looking to set up Ali's magic again. Ali is happy if, when he enters the ring to fight one man, he's actually fighting two—if he is also taking on his next opponent. If the opponent who comes after the opponent you're fighting has a lot of respect for your present opponent, then you're hitting the second man psychologically every time you hit the first one physically. And that builds confidence.

When a man has this kind of confidence, when he can look into future fights, then this man has a certain control over fear. Of course, no fighters admit fear. They call it butterflies or nervousness, or feeling shaky. Still, the kind of pressures fighters get are almost unbearable. But Ali went into a match with positive thinking. He was able to sleep well a week or two before fights, for Ali *knew* he was going to win and nothing can be better than that for a fighter's confidence. It seems true that the more fights you win, the more you're likely to win.

When one's confidence gets really solid, you begin to believe that you can only be defeated by accident.

So I used to worry about the possible accidents in a fight: a butt, a broken hand, and quickly my mind began eliminating them. A butt? My peek-a-boo style prevented the other man from using his head on my face. A broken hand? I could beat any man alive with the other working hand. That was confidence at its peak.

Ali and Dundee had this kind of confidence, or did they know? I was wondering if their confidence was now built on a belief in Ali's magic rather than on the skill of his comeback technique.

CHAPTER 4

December 7, 1970: It is the day of the Ali–Bonavena fight. At twelve Muhammad Ali and Oscar Bonavena are expected to be here. Three hundred people are moving around and they all want to observe the weigh-in. If you don't know that this is part of boxing's long routine, you could think that we are here waiting for the arrival of the President. There at the Felt Forum, a small arena situated to one end of Madison Square Garden, the majority of the crowd is from the press and the media. Every American radio, television, magazine and newspaper seems to have its representative here today. This is the time when both fighters come face to face in boxing trunks, knowing that very soon they'll be throwing leather at each other; the moment when you see the other fighter bigger and stronger than you. And if the other guy shadowboxes and at the end throws a left hook to the air, you see him in better condition than you, and you see the punch he threw harder and faster than any one punch you ever threw. It's painful how your mind amplifies these situations. A fighter suffers in weigh-ins. Some can't even control themselves.

It happened to my last opponent. Minutes before the fight he was substituted for by a friend of mine (who happened to be there wishing me luck at the time the news came my opponent couldn't go on).

The problem had started at the weigh-in ceremony. My rival, after first taking a good look at me, complained of a bad right arm. Then he said it was his left one. The closer I got to him, the more pains and illnesses were uncovered. I knew what was going on. I had often felt the same way when younger, but had had control over my feelings. By fight time my rival had a bad case of diarrhea. I hadn't intended to go that far, but I had literally scared the shit out of him. Believe me, this is a common story and not an isolated one. A fighter on the day of a weigh-in and a fight goes through more than an actor on opening night.

Seeing boxing leeches everywhere I think about these things and I get angry the leeches are here. I can smell them miles away. Can they talk! Sometimes they persuade fighters. They start getting free tickets, then a couple of bucks. By the time you become a top contender you might just as well be addicted to this man. You find yourself asking funny questions, like: "Why am I giving this man two hundred bucks? What is he doing for me?" Yes, these men are here.

Now they talk with each other and with the kind of men that you see only at big fights because they have friends at the Commission's office and at Madison Square Garden; the ones with hangover written on their faces. These are the people with the cigars in their mouths and black hats. They spit on the floor while talking to you. They are the ones who get free loads at the Annual Boxing Writers' Dinner, at fight announcement luncheons, weigh-ins, victory celebrations and bars. These are the types that movie actors like to play in fight films. Well, here they are. Present.

Boxing writers, as usual, are sharing with each other their predictions. And making jokes. Just before fighters show up at weigh-ins the atmosphere is dull, with old boxing people, old boxing commissioners, repeating the same old stories. A retired fighter comes to these weigh-ins and often finds boxing writers asking the same old question: "How do you feel?"

What do they expect one to answer? That you don't feel good? That you are not in shape to return to the ring tomorrow?

Former champions are around. I see Gene Fullmer. A tough man. He was the world's middleweight champ with a style similar to Bonavena's. "Wow!" Gene says, "there are more people here than I saw in all my fights."

Yes, there are many people here. That's why the weigh-in is held here at this large place and not at the Commission's office, where most fighters have their weigh-in ceremony in New York. But this is a big one, and Ali is in it. Ali brings action into every phase of his fights: medical examination, weigh-in, press conferences, the signing of fights, the announcements of fights. There is excitement wherever Ali is.

New York Boxing Commissioner Edwin Dooley is coming in. Only a few notice his presence. He says hello to some of the writers. He is whispering something to John Condon, Garden Publicist. You don't see the chairman at every weigh-in, he's saved for the big ones.

There is some commotion. Writers are walking toward the north side entrance of the Forum. One of the fighters is coming. I can't see. Someone says it's Bonavena. Another group of people are running toward the other side of the ring. I can see both fighters now. Ali is followed by Bundini Brown and Dundee and also a few Black Muslims who keep the crowd at a distance from Ali. Bonavena has two men with him. Both are Spanish, Puerto Ricans. Bonavena had signed with them and these two Puerto Ricans have been the last managers for Bonavena, who seems to have a manager for each of his fights. He doesn't get along with managers.

Just before the fighters' entrance, I was wondering if the Garden people or the commissioners were going to let them be near each other. At the Ali–Quarry weigh-in, the promoters didn't let the fighters be together. They were afraid that Ali, who always puts on a show at weigh-ins, could make a bad scene and spoil the fight.

Of course, promoters and commissioners remember that afternoon in Miami when Cassius Clay came in to the weigh-in and shocked everyone present by staging one of the most emotional put-ons ever done to boxing. At that time, Clay, who had talked himself into the championship bout with Sonny Liston, was the underdog in every betting parlor and in every newspaperman's head. At that time Ali did an incomparable job on Sonny Liston's arrogance. Liston was reduced to saying, "That boy is crazy."

They don't want some of that here. Here is New York, a respectable town engaged in serious business. Of course, here nobody expects a similar confrontation to the one in Miami. Bonavena can't understand too much English and as he told me in Spanish, "Ali talks too fast for me anyhow."

"Chi, chi, chi, chi," Bonavena screams at Ali now that they can see each other. Bonavena extends his right hand and rubs the thumb with a finger and keeps repeating "chi, chi." Now he surprises the audience. "Chicken," he says clearly in English. "Chi, chi, chi."

Everyone seems amazed. But I know what he is doing. Chi, chi is a way to call chicken in Spanish. His extended hand with the rubbing of the fingers means that he has corn in his hand for the chicken. "Chicken," Bonavena repeats, and Ali can't keep from smiling. In a few years, Bonavena has gotten a new word for his English vocabulary. Chicken. But he speaks good Spanish. "Tu eres *maricon*," he says now to Ali who knows what maricon means—queer. His ego, his machismo seems hurt, but he's a pro. He won't show it to us.

Bonavena pinches Ali and repeats the word maricon. Then he calls him "puta" and says, "Black! You stink!" Ali makes unhappy gestures as if Bonavena is crazy. Even through his cool, I can see he's angry.

Ali's traditional script has been tarnished. He was not expecting this kind of competition from Oscar. Ali, whose pre-fight programs always had worked with blacks doesn't seem to know what to do with white fighters. Not with this one, anyway. Bonavena, unlike many of Ali's past black competitors, does not behave in accordance with Ali's script. Bonavena is not taking the supporting actor bit as Ali always expects when he writes his scripts. It could mean trouble.

Nevertheless, Ali, who always sets the stage and tells his actors what particular part to take, had not been able in the past to penetrate white boxers. He didn't even try. He appeared to be stand-offish whenever he met a white man inside the ring. I have a feeling now looking at him smiling at Oscar's remarks, that Ali is aware of his trouble with white fighters. He seems to accept that it is more difficult to psych out a white boxer.

Of course, Ali doesn't necessarily understand his own magic. He said on several occasions that Allah provides him with victories. But one thing is clear when he fights black fighters, he doesn't let Allah do all the work. For Muhammad Ali understands the black man in this country. That's why he psychs them. Ali goes to the root of his people, their culture, their customs, their suffering, their superstitions. It is a profound knowledge of many things that have to do with blacks. Because he understands them and can penetrate their thoughts, they become easier to defeat.

While his latest struggle has been to convince blacks that "black is beautiful," he always knew where to hit black opponents before fights. Some new variant of "black is ugly" is where he would hit them. "White fighters always give me more trouble than 'niggers,'" Ali told me many times.

Looking over the record books I can't find a heavyweight champion who in his first professional fight allowed his first opponent to go the limit. That is with the exception of Muhammad Ali who fought a white ex-cop from West Virginia, a washed-up fighter, who went the full six rounds with Ali. For a time, there seemed little difference in his subjection of white or black fighters, but after becoming champion, Ali again had more trouble with whites than blacks.

In his first defense, he had no difficulty in knocking out Liston in one. Against Patterson, people begged the referee to stop the one-sided match. After the opening round Floyd was fighting with a painful back. It was Canadian George Chuvalo who first gave Ali some trouble. After receiving hard shots to the body, Ali only won the fight by going fifteen tough rounds. Then came England's Henry Cooper who gave Ali trouble until the fight was stopped as a result of an ugly gash over Cooper's eye.

Against Brian London, a live punching bag, Ali had no trouble and knocked him out in three. But against unknown German fighter Karl Mildenberger, Ali had to wait until the seventh round before solving the German's awkward left-handed stance and even then, Ali seemed to keep having trouble until round twelve when Mildenberger fell under a continuous attack from Ali.

Ernie Terrell and Zora Folley, both black, were no contest for the young champion.

These results were not the work of a man who knew the style of these men; their faults or their strong points. He knew something that goes beyond the speed of the punches, beyond one's ability to avoid punches.

But here facing Oscar, Ali seems passive, he doesn't have the witty remarks, the outraged outburst. He is very quiet. Perhaps he smells trouble, perhaps he's not worried, perhaps he's saving his energy for tonight.

I think that the three-and-a-half years he was off made a different man out of him. His behavior is similar to that shown in Atlanta. Is it because he has fallen in another bag, or is it because the Black Muslims warn him off from psyching white devils?

Well, he probably doesn't want to waste words and witty remarks on a man who wouldn't understand them. For his part, Bonavena doesn't care. He talks Spanish to Ali as if Ali understands him . . . or the reporters, who with the exception of three of us, don't understand Spanish either.

This weigh-in ceremony is nothing in comparison with Ali's previous ones in Miami with Liston, in Las Vegas with Floyd or in Houston with Terrell. Condon announces Ali's weight as 212; Bonavena's as 204.

The ceremony is over and both fighters are leaving Felt Forum. They are going back to their respective hotels to pretend they are going to rest.

Now the thinking, the real thinking begins. Now the fighters will picture how the fight is going to go. Bonavena, the proud Argentinean, full of machismo, will probably picture his victory with Argentina going crazy. It is really something to dream about a victory over Ali. He is the most important athlete since Joe Louis.

Ali will have people in his room and he'll be talking and demonstrating, against an invisible opponent, how Bonavena is going to fall. That's the way Ali releases his tension.

Will he start the fight by doing the same thing he did with Quarry? Go all out in the first?

CHAPTER 5

Muhammad Ali has done it again. You can't get one more soul in this place. And when Madison Square Garden is full of people, the excitement is outrageous. And then, Ali brings a special crowd to his fights. There are more blacks here dressed with fancy clothes than there were in Atlanta, but somehow they look less conspicuous. New York changes scenes.

If you go by the ringside seats and begin to ask people what's a jab, a right cross, or an uppercut, they might think you are talking about drinks. Many ringside people come here to show off. Others to pretend. Seventy-five dollars for a ringside seat! The place is full of people, people who can afford to be here and people who will not eat for the next few days, and people who pawned their best jewelry just to be here tonight.

Argentineans living in New York seem to be all here and they are chanting from two different sections. They are sitting a few rows back of the ringside seats.

Oddly enough, this crowd reminds me of the people who only come to Golden Gloves; a special crowd. They can name you any of the Golden Gloves champions in any given year.

I won the New York Golden Gloves in 1958 and I went to the 1966 Golden Gloves finals in the old Madison Square Garden, and people began to remind me about that wonderful year when I won the tournament. Then they would ask, "What ever happened to you? Did you quit the game?" Not knowing that I'd just won the *world's* light heavyweight crown a few months before.

Something like that characterizes the crowd we have here now. They only come to big events, and as in the Golden Gloves where whites root for whites, and blacks for black fighters rather than dividing on which side they bet their money, so, tonight, you can tell whites will be rooting for Oscar.

I'm sitting in the fifth row, behind the press row and Ali looks good from here. Bonavena walks around and waves to some of his countrymen who come toward the ring to tell him in Spanish how to beat Ali. "Ringo," one of them screams at Bonavena, "keep on top of him and throw punches. You're too strong for him." Bonavena shakes his head yes. Smiles. Many people call Bonavena, Ringo, because his hairdo is similar to the Beatles' Ringo. And Bonavena, like a few other fighters, Muhammad Ali included, has joined the music world and has made some recordings in Argentina.

Here the music is different; if you are to play good music, you have to maintain the rhythm yourself and spoil the other man's rhythm. I bet that Ali won't be able to keep his rhythm. Bonavena won't let him. As referee Mark Conn gives the instructions, Ali's lips move. Maybe Angelo taught Ali some Spanish. Bonavena smiles though the mouthpiece. I look at both fighters' stomachs and like with every other fighter, they tremble. Both fighters move their bodies as if to keep warm, but as they listen to the referee's instructions, they move to relieve the pressure. Now they walk back to their respective corners.

Ali stops, faces his corner, extends both hands, palms up. Now he closes his eyes and begins to pray. The man with the bell seems to be waiting for Ali to end his Black Muslim ritual. As Ali's hands move down and his body turns toward the ring, the bell rings. Again, I feel that funny feeling in my stomach.

Ali walks to the middle of the ring, now slides to his left and feints. Bonavena's body moves down to evade the punch that never came. Now Ali slides to his right. He is moving good and seems in control. Everyone is quiet.

Bonavena rushes Ali. Ali moves back and makes a swift move to his left and feints again. Bonavena's short arms move to block the punch that should have gone to his face. There was no punch to block. Ali smiles. Bonavena rushes again and throws a wild left hook. Ali steps back.

Ali seems in control. And he looks good while moving with class, sometimes by the book. Bonavena now runs toward Ali like a bull attacking the bullfighter. Ali, just like a banderillero, moves to one side and instead of putting in the sticks simply pushes Bonavena against the ropes and heaves Bonavena's head between the third and fourth ropes. Ali is signaling the Argentinean that the ring is here, not there.

Bonavena comes back. He is mad. People laugh and the Argentineans chant in Spanish: "Rin—go. Rin—go."

Bonavena charges Ali again. This time Ali gets hit with punches that appear to have hit him below the belt. Ali stops to complain. The referee signals Bonavena to bring his punches up. Bonavena shakes his head and walks toward Ali who moves continuously. I didn't like Ali's complaint to the referee. That's lack of professionalism. A boxer is there to do the fighting. It's the referee's job to restrain any man he sees who accidentally or purposely breaks the rules.

As the bell ends the first round, Ali makes a military about-face and Bonavena walks sloppily toward his corner.

I'm getting ready to walk toward the press row to give my friend Pete Hamill some of my quick impressions of the first round and I hear a man saying: "That fuckin' Argentinean looks like a fire hydrant. And walks like one."

Many writers bang at their typewriters as I kneel to whisper to Hamill that perhaps the six to one odds in favor of Ali are justified. Obviously, I had thought that the ones responsible for those odds were crazy.

I discussed the fight with Pete many times before tonight, and now Pete seems to have a question mark on his face. "The old Ali is back," Pete says. I nod yes.

The ten-second whistle sends me back to my seat. Angelo is now leaning against the ropes and whispers instructions to Ali. In the other corner Oscar says yes with his head at everything his trainer says.

The bell. Audience is more relaxed now. You can hear some noises. Everyone is analyzing the fight. My two younger brothers just came down from their cheap seats to kneel in the aisle beside me. Both are amateur fighters. One, Rambert, is rooting for Ali. The other, Tony, wants Bonavena to win. The Spanish blood, he had explained. I have two brothers here. One thinks like a white tonight, the other like a black.

In the ring Ali maintains his posture. He is the king. Bonavena keeps trying to penetrate Ali who moves as in the previous round, and presents a difficult target.

A jab. Another one. Now he moves back. Ali is good tonight. Was I wrong! Ali throws a one-two combination and both punches land on Oscar's head. Rambert jumps up to applaud. I look at some white faces ringside and they seem to be resigned to another victory for the "loud mouth."

The bell catches Ali evading a wild left hook and a roundhouse right hand.

Whites are quiet and so is my brother Tony. Ali is handling Bonavena like a baby. The old moves have come back to Ali and he's going to be a tough man to defeat tonight. True, Oscar has landed a few shots that would never have hit Ali at his best, but still in comparison with the Quarry fight, Ali seems to be ready for Frazier, the other man in the ring tonight. Ali is probably looking at Frazier in his mind instead of at Oscar.

At the bell, Pete looks back and gives me the victory sign. We are pulling for Ali.

Now it is the third round and Ali begins to do exactly as he did in the previous two rounds. He moves and flicks left jabs. Oscar also does exactly as he did in rounds one and two, he charges, sometimes with control, most times with anger. One thing he does which I think many of us so-called smart fighters never do: he misses and keeps trying. He misses some more and keeps trying. He doesn't get frustrated. Any change in Ali's pattern and then we would see why Bonavena tries and tries and tries.

Oscar keeps up the pressure. He swings stiff punches like a madman. What patience! Bonavena seems to be saying to himself: "Don't worry, we'll catch up." And he charges again. The elusive Ali still moves like in the first. He pushes Oscar around. Oscar charges. Ali steps to the side and pushes Oscar again. Pressure doesn't seem to bother Ali as I had expected, although he himself is not punching much.

Of course I expect Ali to be a little slower in later rounds, but I expect the same from Oscar. So their deterioration will be relative. Which means that Ali will win this fight going away. I see no reason why Ali should change his pattern.

Ali misses a good right. Very seldom does Ali lead with a right, but he did. It looked good, even missing. A left jab hits Oscar.

Ali backs off. Ali throws two fast jabs. Oscar bends and hits Ali in the belly. Ali moves away toward his corner and now turns his back to Oscar and walks two steps to his corner with the sound of the bell.

"There is no way for Bonavena to beat Ali," Rambert says to me and Tony. "He's something tonight. Better than ever." Tony doesn't answer. I make believe I can't hear. "I told you," Rambert continues, "Ali is Ali."

There is not much excitement. The fight is going as expected. Ali is playing with Oscar and blacks are relaxed. They are winning too. So they simply enjoy the evening. Ali's victories win more than simple fights inside rings. Blacks are conspicuously quiet. No words are necessary when their man is doing it with his fists a few feet away. So the lack of excitement is a combination of the disappointment of Bonavena's followers and the comfortable acceptance of Ali's crowd.

We can all hear the bell to start the fourth. Again, there goes Oscar. He wants to hit and be hit. His hands are lower than before. Ali jabs and crosses with a right. The jab hits. The right cross misses. Oscar walks in. A left hook is blocked by Ali. Oscar throws another hook, again Ali blocks it. Ali is not moving like before. He is no longer on his toes. Now they are both in the middle of the ring, and for the first time they get inside. Man-to-man. They in-fight. Ali has changed.

Rambert looks at Tony. Tony looks straight into the ring. Ali is being hit in the body. He remains inside. Bonavena is happy. The movable target has stopped. Bonavena smiles. His man is right in there with him. The latter part of the Quarry second round is back with Ali.

He is now against the ropes and Bonavena pounds away. The crowd is on their feet. This action is Bonavena's first threat to

Ali's dominance. The sleeping crowd has awakened. The white man is hitting the nigger.

However, Bonavena's punches don't make contact with Ali's vulnerable spots. Not yet.

Ali has given up something under the continuous pressure. I think it's a matter of confidence. Hamill turns his head to look at me. Rambert jumps up and shouts instructions at Ali. Tony smiles while he fixes his glasses. Happy white faces surround us. The Argentineans come alive. In fact, they are running around with the special cops pushing them back to their seats. Now the Argentineans chant again. Some of the whites chant with them.

Bonavena is banging Ali. Ali blocks a wicked left hook to his right side with his elbow. Bonavena connects with a looping right to Ali's face. You don't see this too often. Ali's face touched? Another right lands on his face. Ali now tries to move out of the ropes and Bonavena pushes him back. Bonavena punches furiously. Bonavena the unorthodox is throwing crazy punches. He punches down. He pulls one hand back and punches with the other. He extends his left for measurement and shoots the wildest uppercut I've ever seen. Bonavena uses his peculiar, strange style. It is not that he is unpredictable; we know that he is going to throw these types of punches. The trouble is that fighters are not used to standing in front of awkward swings.

Ali throws a flurry of punches. Not hard, just to distract Oscar who seems impossible to distract. Oscar has his chin down, against his chest, and keeps punching at Ali. Some of the punches miss, some don't. The bell. People applaud the fighters. "The people liked this round," Tony mumbles to Rambert. "Bullshit," Rambert says, "these whiteys want Ali to get killed." Tony laughs and I go to see Pete.

"He's tired," Pete tells me. "I think he's in trouble."

"He is not tired. He is losing confidence," I say.

An English writer in the next seat agrees with Pete. "No doubt," the English writer says, "Ali is tired."

For a man supposedly in top physical condition, Ali should not be tired. He has no reason to be tired. He is an old pro, and old pros don't succumb to pressures and that's all Bonavena is giving. Ali's confidence is what is affected. He is disconcerted because Bonavena has not been paying attention to Ali's punches. Oscar comes right back. Only one thing is pushing Ali to the ropes and that's frustration. For three rounds, Ali pulled and pushed and kept himself away from the ropes. Why now?

It is not that Bonavena is getting better. Oscar is unchangeable. He does the same thing over and over, he just waits for his rival to "get tired" or waits until his man gives up. You check Bonavena's record and you can understand why thirty-seven of his forty-five opponents have not been able to finish on their feet. Bonavena's refusal to step back is a good formula; a good compensation for the stillness of his brain.

One thing is sure, Bonavena no longer looks like the six-to-one underdog. Don't forget, if Bonavena connects good he might finish this fight. It was not for kicks that he knocked George Chuvalo down. In fact, he has been the only man to drop the Canadian.

Forty seconds have passed in the fifth round. It is a copy of round four. Ali is now against the ropes again. Oscar is striking everything; arms and gloves, body and head. A tremendous right chop misses Ali by an inch. People make sounds of amazement. Bonavena stands square in front of Ali, his body pushing forward, his hands moving from every angle toward no particular spot. Bonavena just wants to make contact with any part of Ali's body. Ali seems to look for a rest. Oscar doesn't let him.

Ali throws a soft flurry of punches, each one hits Bonavena around his head. It provokes no change. Bonavena keeps coming. Ali remains against the ropes. A right by Bonavena hits Ali flush on the mouth. There is the bell and Oscar throws one more right that misses.

Rambert is shouting instructions to Ali who is now sitting on his stool, breathing hard. Angelo doesn't stop talking. Bundini Brown is massaging Ali's back with a wet sponge. They are obviously worried. Bonavena has probably won the last two rounds.

In the Garden, the sense of commotion is building. I can feel it in the seats. There is no longer the quietness of the first three rounds. I feel the commotion. Round six begins. Silence.

Bonavena comes to Ali. Ali waits for him with a jab. A right. Another jab. Ali is close to the ropes again. Ali says something to Oscar. Oscar smiles. Ali throws one, two, three jabs. Now a left hook and a right. The right hits Bonavena on the forehead. I couldn't see if the left hook made contact. Bonavena chases Ali, who moves backward and to the side. Ali has become again, as in the first three rounds, a moving target. Hard to connect. Oscar keeps walking in patiently waiting for Ali to stop.

But now Ali stops only to throw punches. Oscar tries to counter, but Ali is not there. Oscar keeps up the pressure. Ali moves, not as fast as he once did, but moving fast enough to prevent Oscar from coming close. Ali punches and moves. He is doing it beautifully.

When a boxer punches, the other one concentrates on evading the punches. If you punch and move, by the time your opponent gets set you are not there. Ali is doing that now.

Tony complains. I don't know why but people are booing Ali. "This Bonavena is dumb," Tony says. "He's following Ali around. He should cut the ring short." Ten seconds to go and

Bonavena charges. Ali is too far from Bonavena to hit him or to be hit. Ali throws a one-two combination which misses over Oscar's head. Both fighters get inside for the first time in this round. The bell catches the referee as he separates the fighters.

Not many punches were thrown in the last round. I score for Ali. It was a dull round, the dullest so far, but I thought Ali was coming back to being himself. He's probably doing what he did to Mildenberger. Took his time to figure the German out. He might be doing the same with Oscar.

If he does, it would be impressive. With Bonavena you have to content yourself with hitting him once in a while and keeping away from his attacks. You can't waste time working out a plan for Oscar. This man is impossible!

That was the bell for round seven. Bonavena comes out slowly. Ali meets him. A right, a hard one, hits Oscar just below his forehead. Ali throws a left hook, another right, steps back and comes in again with a jab–right cross combination. Oscar tries to counter but Ali returns a hard left hook, and a right uppercut that catches Bonavena on the chin. Bonavena's mouthpiece flies in the air. Ali hits and his punches seem fast and hard. Ali steps back, as if to watch Oscar falling down.

Oscar smiles again. He maintains the same pace. Nothing has happened. Indestructible Oscar keeps coming in. Ali moves. I look straight at Ali and he seems worried. Bonavena is charging and the clock says that there are forty seconds left to the end of the round. Ali is against the ropes. Bonavena forgets about Ali's face, and throws every punch to Ali's body.

Many times when a fighter gets hit on any part of the face there is no pain. But if you want to give pain to your rival, the thing to do is to hit him in the body: in the hanging ribs, in the solar plexus, in the liver. It is painful and many times scary.

I've hit fighters in their bodies with so much force that they couldn't help but let out an involuntary groan like a wounded wolf. Usually the man who connects will jump at the hurt fighter with more punches. I never attacked after such a punch. I used to step back and let my rival savor every second of pain. I was not only a sadist but a technician; I know how discouraging those punches were to the body. I became world's champion by throwing one. A left hook to the liver.

So, that's probably what Bonavena is doing now. He seems desperate as he pounds in all kinds of punches to Ali's body. Ali is leaning on the ropes, making every effort to diminish the force of the punches. His elbows block many, but some of Bonavena's uppercuts are getting through.

I run toward Pete. "He's in trouble," I say. Pete watches closely and nods his head. "He can't figure this guy out," Pete answers as he looks at the action in the ring. A wild Bonavena hook lands in Ali's hanging ribs at the bell. Close round but I think Ali won it.

Tony stays in my seat while Rambert comes to the press row to analyze the fight with Pete, the English writer, and me.

The only trouble with analyzing fights is that I have to do all the talking. "Ali is in serious danger of losing," I begin. "Tricks don't work with Bonavena and the more tricks Ali tries, the more frustrated he gets. He has to stop that. The only thing he can do is move and punch; punch and move. If he wants to trick him, that's the trick to use. The only trick." I look at my pad. I have Ali winning rounds one, two, three, six and seven. But Oscar's pressure is starting to pay off.

"Move, Ali," I shout. Bundini signals me not to worry.

While we wait for round eight, I'm thinking this is a very important round. Ali had predicted on a television show that

Oscar was going to fall in nine. So he'll probably come out throwing more leather to soften Oscar. If he's going for the kill in round nine, he has to do some mollifying in the eighth. My thoughts are disturbed by the bell. Round eight.

Surprisingly, Bonavena is the one who increases the attack. Ali tries to move back. He can't. Bonavena is swinging terrific shots to Ali's body. The crowd stands. Oscar is punching with fury. He pushes Ali. He has Ali against the ropes again. Once more, Ali is in trouble. A special cop is pulling me and my brother from the press row. No one is allowed to scream from the press rows and we are going wild shouting instructions to Ali and yelling at him to move. I want Ali to do the same thing he did in the first couple of rounds; to move to the side and to push Oscar toward the ropes. Tony screams that Ali is too tired. "Bonavena has the victory in his pocket," Tony says.

Bonavena pounds on Ali. Ali becomes the stationary target again. He is there for Bonavena to swing at him. Fifteen seconds to go and Bonavena is having a party with Ali. Oscar throws a flurry. The bell. Big round for Bonavena.

"This is the round," Rambert says. "Ali will knock this guy's brains out."

"What fight are you watching?" asks Tony.

One thing we should all expect. Ali is going to try to fulfill his prediction. The first time he had been embarrassed was in New York, in the old Madison Square Garden. The night he predicted he was going to knock Doug Jones out in six. He failed and won a very close decision. He might try harder this time. But so far, Ali is getting the worst of the exchanges. And we all know that Ali doesn't like to get hit.

The bell for the ninth.

Blacks stand up. No one dares to complain. If a black is blocking your view, get up too. Can't complain.

Ali charges. A right hits Oscar. Ali is flat-footed. He's looking for power. A jab and a right hit Oscar again on his face. Oscar misses. Ali connects with a tremendous right to Oscar's chin. Bonavena is stunned. Ali is really trying to end the fight now.

Perfect shots like the one that just hit Oscar tend to give one a feeling of thousands of ants running through one's body. One loses control over legs and hands momentarily. This feeling lasts for perhaps one to three seconds. We call it being shook up.

Ali goes for the kill. His perceptive eyes have seen what many of us saw. Wow! Bonavena just hit Ali coming in. Bonavena is throwing rights and lefts to Ali who seems hurt by Oscar's right. Ali fights back now. An exchange. Both fighters are connecting. They are swapping terrific punches. Strangely, Bonavena is against the ropes. They are still swinging. Oh! Indestructible Bonavena is down. Half of his stocky body is outside the ropes. Referee Conn says there was no knockdown. It was a slip. Oscar's gloves are being cleaned by Conn. Ali comes. The trade continues. A wild left by Oscar. Ali is almost down, and the crowd is up on their feet.

What a round! The fighters are still in there and they are punching savagely at each other. It's hard to describe every punch, but Ali has never been hit like this before. Oscar and Ali both seem tired. Oscar connects. Now Ali comes back with a left hook–right cross combination. Not too much power. There is the bell. Both fighters are swinging. Referee Conn breaks them apart. About six punches are thrown after the bell. It was an even round. No, I think Ali won it. Close.

Ali is wrong again. People boo. Argentineans chant again. Bonavena had one little victory. Ali's predicted round is over and *he* was the one who almost got knocked out. I've never seen Ali hurt this much. He was in bad shape. He showed guts. All those so-called experts who always said that Ali had no balls have just been proven wrong. Of course, I think Ali was wrong in trying to accomplish his prediction. Amateurs do that. But perhaps he had his reasons.

My two brothers are happy. They both predict that their favorite is going to win. And they're saying that the other man was at the edge of being knocked out. They are both right.

Believe me, four years ago this would have never happened. Ali's head is not right. How can this happen? How can a fighter like Bonavena, whose only major ingredient is toughness, give Ali so much trouble? Something must be wrong with Ali.

Round ten just started. Bonavena is pressing but not with the same drive as before. Ali is backing up flat-footed. A turtle follows a turtle. Twenty-five seconds have passed and not a single punch has been thrown. Both fighters are showing the effect of the blows they traded in the previous round. They are saving energy. Ali throws a lazy jab. Bonavena slowly increases the attack. Ali is tired. The crowd is now pulling for Bonavena again. But Oscar seems weary. They are both coasting, trying to recover. Four hundred and sixteen pounds struggling together, looking to recover every muscle and nerve. Having been pounded over and over, it is not an easy thing to recover in one minute.

People boo Ali who moves back slowly with Oscar chasing him drowsily. No style now. Ali just walks backward. When Bonavena makes a move, Ali extends both his arms. This round is much worse than the sixth. Ali keeps walking sloppily back. Oscar follows like a drunken bear.

Physical tiredness has a limit. When a fighter is in good physical condition he tends to breathe fast the first minute he encounters physical effort. Then he reaches a balance and can punch and move and punch and even get hit, but his level of tiredness is not affected. For Oscar that seems to be the case. He can't get more tired than he is now. I have my doubts about Ali, however, because Ali's confidence is involved here. When confidence is affected, the level of tiredness starts being determined by the mind not the body.

Of course, one is exhausted after a fight is over. That's to be expected. A fighter can enter the ring at ten one night, and knock his opponent out in one round. At twelve, the winner is going to be "dead tired" and not because of the energy he used in the ring, but because the tension of two or three months' training is leaving his head and body.

But the assumption here is that if this fight keeps going on the way it is now, Ali will be more tired than Oscar.

In the ring there is no action. People boo Ali. He's causing the dullness of the fight. He is also preventing Oscar from connecting solid blows. Professional Ali doesn't let the crowd bother him. He should be well ahead on the score cards.

There is the bell and people boo. I think the judges might give the round to Oscar. But it was about even.

Round eleven finds Ali leaning against the ropes. Oscar is throwing awkward punches to Ali's body. Ali tries to push Bonavena but as far as Ali is concerned, Bonavena now weights two tons. Bonavena, this far along in the fight is one heavy mass. Oscar is shoving his body through Ali's extended arms. Not a punch has been thrown by Ali. He is tired.

Bonavena is doing the pushing now. He sneaks a left to the body. Bonavena takes a look at the clock. Twenty seconds are left until the end of this dull round. Bonavena opens up with lefts and rights to Ali's still body. The bell. And people applaud. Another Bonavena round.

It goes on like that. The thirteenth is like the twelfth and the fourteenth like the thirteenth.

Three rounds have passed. I'm looking at my pad, and it makes me nervous. I have Ali ahead seven to six, with round ten even. Of the last five rounds I have given Ali only one, the thirteenth, and that one was close. Ali seems to be hanging there. His magic is not working.

Rounds twelve and fourteen were easily Oscar's rounds. Similar to the eleventh. A big fifteenth round for Oscar could provide a tremendous upset, as far as boxing experts are concerned.

At the bell, both fighters walk slowly toward the center of the ring. Conn makes them touch gloves. It is a tradition. The touch of the gloves for the last round.

Bonavena charges, Ali moves back. They both seem a little fresher. They know it's the last round. They're probably prepared to go all out. Bonavena throws a wild hook, then launches a right, and Ali steps back and jabs. Bonavena keeps the pressure on. He feels he can win this fight if he can capture this round convincingly. He throws another right that lands on Ali's left shoulder. Bonavena is hunting. The round is one minute old. Ali tries to move on his toes. Bonavena presses. Bonavena jabs. Bonavena walks menacingly to Ali. He throws another of his awkward left hooks. Ali pulls back. Bonavena prepares to shoot a right. Ali waits. Bonavena telegraphs his right. Ali steps in with a wicked left hook. It beats Oscar's right. Oscar's legs wobble. Indestructible Bonavena is going down! His eyes stare at the ring lights. His body falls. Bonavena is badly hurt. He is up, his eyes are glassy. He's up, but his legs refuse to stay straight. Ali is coming. Ali hits. He doesn't seem tired now. Ali is connecting. Oscar's body is down again.

Referee Conn does not send Ali to a neutral corner and Ali happily remains close to Oscar, who is now struggling to get up. Oscar's body is rolling. He's walking like a wounded dog. Arms and legs move on the floor as he tries to stand up. Conn follows him counting with mouth and with fingers.

A towel is thrown into the ring. It came from the direction of Oscar's corner. Powerful Bonavena is finally up. I think Conn counted to nine. Ali is right on top. A left hook and a right hit Bonavena on the forehead. Bonavena is out on his feet. Another left by Ali. Bonavena is down. The fight is over. It's a technical knockout; three knockdowns in one round and the fight is automatically over.

The magic of Ali. The magic of Ali. Nothing else. Indestructible Oscar is looking, but not looking at Ali who moves with his hands high and now embraces Bundini. The fight is over. Just when every black in the place thought that Ali was finished, he came back. To a dull, unexciting match, Ali provided a fantastic ending. It has to be the magic of Ali. What else?

One of the worst fights in which Ali has been involved became an interesting match in two minutes and three seconds of the last round.

That quick, unexpected left hook by Ali is going to convince many people to think that Frazier—who in fact is a hard guy to hit clean—will be easy to take out with that type of punch. Ali shouldn't listen to them. Ali should try to get his confidence back by fighting a couple of stiffs. But, of course, he is going on to Frazier next.

CHAPTER 6

Joe Frazier is a deceptive fighter. You can see him trading punches with another boxer and think he is a heavyweight with no class and no style. Like Marciano, Joe Frazier deceives people. He is one of those rare heavyweights, who is able to use himself to his maximum potential. This is what has made Frazier an undefeated heavyweight champion of the world, scoring twenty-three knockouts in a total of twenty-six fights.

His nickname "Smokin' Joe" is an appropriate description. "When I get into a ring it's to fight and not fool around," he says. "And my opponent better understand that. When he is fighting me, he's *fighting*, not playing."

The first time I saw him in action was against Bonavena on September 21, 1966. After watching Frazier go to the floor twice, get up, keep his cool, and eventually win, I saw a man with the right boxing attitude.

Eight months later I saw Frazier again. This time he pummeled George Chuvalo so consistently that the referee stopped the match with the Canadian "out on his feet."

Then on March 4, 1968, eleven months after New York Boxing Commissioner Dooley took Ali's title away for Ali's refusal to be inducted in the U.S. Army, the same Commissioner sanctioned a "world's championship match" between Buster Mathis and the undefeated Frazier.

At the time, I was in training camp with Mathis. We boxed together and I was impressed with Buster (who had once beaten Frazier when they were both in the amateur ranks). Mathis knew every punch in the book. And he carried a good wallop.

I said to myself that Frazier was going to be in for a surprise. I felt that Mathis had the necessary tools to provide the strong man from Philadelphia with an upset. Besides, I didn't think "Smokin' Joe" had forgotten their amateur encounter.

I saw Buster beating Frazier in the Olympic trials held in New York in 1963 and Buster had simply outpointed Frazier by moving out of the way for three rounds.

This time, Buster did the same thing. He moved and moved, sticking left jabs out, throwing a flurry of punches once in a while and then moving away. And, with me yelling instructions from the floor, Buster easily won five of the first six rounds. But "Smokin' Joe" kept smoking. He maintained the pressure. He kept coming in swinging hard, fast punches. From the seventh round on, the contest became very tough. Frazier survived, Mathis didn't. In round eleven, Frazier threw a left hook to Buster's ribs, followed up with a chopping right to Buster's head, and all of Buster's two hundred and forty pounds fell. He dropped more from the pressure than the power of Frazier's punches. Buster stayed on the canvas until the referee counted him out.

When Frazier destroyed Jerry Quarry on June 23, 1969, in seven rounds, in his fourth defense of the title, the man was ready. Frazier had become championship material. He was a hard man to nail with clean shots, and he was not getting hit like before. That's when I started to worry about Muhammad Ali.

Eight months later, Frazier ruined Ali's sparring partner, Jimmy Ellis, in four rounds. This time, because Ellis was called the world's champion by the World Boxing Association, Frazier gained worldwide recognition for his crown.

Again, Ellis couldn't hit Frazier, who moved in bobbing and weaving and throwing punches from a crouch. It was Frazier at his best. Now the experts began comparing him with greats from the past, and there were a wad of stories about his biography and they were all the same. He had the kind of life and career you described just one way. Born on a farm near Beaufort, South Carolina, on January 13, 1944, Frazier's ambition was to be a meat cutter. But at seventeen, following his older brothers and sister up North, a kid weighing almost two hundred and fifty pounds, he decided to lose some weight in the gym.

He became a fighter. A tough one. Under the eye of Yancey "Yank" Durham, who was a trainer at the P.A.L. in Philadelphia, the young apprentice meat cutter began that long struggle with its huge payoff.

Boxing became Joe Frazier's way to make a living. A job. There was no romanticism involved, no ideals, not a way to advance his people. Boxing was his livelihood. And he went at it with tremendous desire.

He was a professional boxer the way someone else is a skilled carpenter, a painter or doctor. Frazier didn't distract his thoughts with anything else. He shared his boxing with nothing. He just worked to get his body in shape and his mind in condition.

Now Joe Frazier, with his mind and body in championship working condition, was training to fight Muhammad Ali. I would think of Frazier working at his trade, and how he loves his work, especially when he's getting two and a half million dollars to go into the same ring with Muhammad Ali. It would be a pleasure for him to make that bunch of money, but it seems to be equally important to get Ali to fall under his power.

Of course, I don't think Ali can beat Frazier. I don't think so, because of Ali's immediate past performances. I saw crucial flaws in his last two fights. Flaws that would fit perfectly into Frazier's style. If you don't have full confidence and you don't have a hundred percent of will and desire to use your full physical capacities then you are in bad trouble with Joe Frazier.

With Ali's mind working at his best, and with only seventy-five percent of his physical qualities, I would have no doubts he could beat Frazier. But in Atlanta Ali was only twenty percent at his worst, perhaps fifty percent of himself at his best. With Bonavena he was no more than forty percent. With that kind of average I couldn't see how he could beat Frazier.

"Smokin' Joe" has always given a hundred percent of himself. That means that Frazier's confidence and will is always there with him. In my boxing arithmetic, the hundred percent of confidence and will is sixty-five percent of physical fitness and that makes him a tough human being to beat. Especially when this perfect machine has a head to go with it. For Joe Frazier is, to use one of Ali's favorite phrases, "not as dumb as he looks." So, while Frazier's hundred percent is not better than Ali's hundred percent, Joe uses his. Ali doesn't.

I remember when I first met Frazier, after his victory over Mathis. "You know," he said, "I saw you shouting numbers at Buster." I laughed. Frazier was referring to the key I had with Buster to tell him which punches to throw. I would call out numbers and Mathis would jab or hook, uppercut or work on throwing his right. Frazier continued: "You yell 'one, two, six seven eight,' and I hit him nine, ten, eleven, twelve."

Next time I saw Joe was in a fight that my stablemate, world's lightweight champion Ismael Laguna, had in Philadelphia. Frazier was pulling for the other guy.

We spoke for a while but I never told him how much I respected him, and how much I admired his boxing ability and his exceptional ability to be serious in my business.

Probably he thought I didn't like him and never understood why I always cheered against him. But I was friendly with Bonavena; Buster was my stablemate; and Ali was a man I respected as a fighter, a friend, and a man who would undergo psychological pain for his ideas.

That's why I wanted Ali to be the heavyweight king. Yet, though I wanted Ali to win, I wrote on different occasions that I thought Frazier would be too much for him.

About this time, six weeks before the "Fight of the Century" between Ali and Frazier, I was approached by the Publisher of *Boxing Illustrated*, Bert Randolph Sugar. He wanted me to do a book on Muhammad Ali. I was full of my experiences watching the Quarry and Bonavena fights, full of the frustration of not being a fighter myself anymore and tempted. I only thought about it a couple of days before I agreed. I knew that to do a biography of Muhammad Ali would depend to some extent on newspaper material and old feature stories, and from my own experiences with them, I knew how false that was. But I had the advantage of knowing most of the people in Ali's camp, and I was confident I could get the interviews. So I began.

And the research began. Bert Sugar hired a girl to transcribe tape recorder interviews, and to aid him in looking up old papers and old magazines. I began to interview people who knew Ali.

I flew to Miami where Ali was training and spoke with him. I never told him I was doing a book. But once, after a one-hour interview Ali said: "José, I hope you don't use this in the U.S. because I'm doing my book with Richard Durham and no one knows the story I've just told you."

An hour later I went back to Puerto Rico to figure out how I would tell my friend Ali that I was doing a book about him. I flew back to Miami four days later and told him I was writing the book about him, and that if he didn't want any part of what he had already told me in the book to tell me. "That's O.K.," he said. And I interviewed him four more times.

What follows are some chapters from Ali's life. As you will see, a lot of it is in interviews, and a lot, unfortunately, refers to fights I never saw and am describing by what fight reporters saw. Since they sometimes see nothing, I am in the funny position of not always being able to interpret fights that went into the making of a great career. And a lot of what you will see of Ali is contradictory. But then he is a contradictory man and as complex as anybody I've ever known. Let us see how much better an idea we get of him from taking a look at his life before we go on to watch him with Frazier on their historic night, March 8, 1971.

PART II

CHAPTER 7

L ate in Capricorn, coming near to Aquarius, Cassius Clay (six pounds, seven ounces) was born in Louisville at 6:35 P.M. on January 17, 1942. The earliest thing Clay remembers is "walking down the street, getting off a bus with my mother and father on the way to our new house, which was the one I was raised in from four years to eighteen. I remember going down the street," he told me, "and in that yard and climbing up an apple tree and a man telling me to get out before you break a leg and I got down and ran back through the house—with no furniture in it.

"At one time our people were poor financially," Clay said. "But we was rich with health, rich with friends. I always been happy because I always knew what I wanted to do and that's to be heavyweight champion.

"I started boxing because I thought this was the fastest way for a black person to make it in this country. I was not that bright and quick in school, couldn't be a football or a basketball player 'cause you have to go to college and get all kinds of degrees and pass examinations. A boxer can just go to a gym, jump around, turn professional, win a fight, get a break, and he is in the ring.

If he's good enough he makes more money than ballplayers make all their lives."

Six weeks after first stepping inside Joe Martin's gym at the age of twelve, Clay won his first amateur fight. A year later, Clay was fighting on TV, and already collecting a large Louisville following for his amateur fights by going on a door-to-door canvassing tour to tell his neighbors that he was going to "whup" someone on the tube.

But Clay had been magnetizing attention long before he went to Joe Martin's gym. "I've been an attraction ever since I been able to walk and talk," Clay says. "When I was just a little boy in school, I caught on to how nearly everybody likes to watch somebody that acts different. Like, I wouldn't ride the school bus, I would run to school alongside it, and all the kids would be waving and hollering at me, calling me nuts. It makes me somebody special. Or at recess time I'd start a fight with somebody to draw a crowd. I always liked to draw crowds."

Clay never *had* to work. His father always made enough to provide for his family. For more than twenty years he was one of Louisville's most successful sign painters. Always confident of his success, Clay, Sr. bought his first home when he was twenty-three. He boasts that he was never out of work one day in his life, "and I never worked for nobody but me."

But when the father was not painting, he was sometimes drinking or he was fighting. The Police Department's record on Clay, Sr. shows that he was arrested four times for reckless driving, twice for disorderly conduct, once for ignoring parking tickets, and once for disposing of mortgaged property. Twice he was arrested on charges of assault and battery. On three different occasions, according to writer Bob Waters, his wife had to call the police. "Heck, it's easy to get into a little scrape," the elder Clay said. "But let them show where I've ever spent even one night in jail . . . they can't do it."

Cassius Clay, Sr. is a man who dresses fancy and doesn't hide his interest in females. "My father is a hep-cat," said Clay, Jr. "He is a hep fella—fifty-seven years old crazy about the girls. He can't ride down the street without turning around. He outlooks me. He'll go around the block four times if he sees a girl. He likes nice, heavyset ladies around a hundred ninety-five pounds . . . calls them 'stallions.' "

Clay tells the following story about his father. "One day in Kentucky when I was a little boy and didn't understand how pretty ladies were, he jumped out of the car and caught a bus. I wondered why he caught the bus. He rode the bus a half-a-mile and got off. He came back telling me: 'I just wanted this girl's phone number.'

"My daddy is a playboy. He is always wearing white shoes and pink pants and blue shirts, and he says he'll never get old.

"He's just like another of the fellas. He's just a brother, more brother than a daddy, and we have a lot of fun. He is a sign painter. He's an artist. He's been painting signs all his life. He raised us painting signs. Another thing about my father . . . that's why I talk so much—cause he outtalks me!"

One time Mr. Clay was driving his car in the company of a girl, Marion Dorsey, when they were both arrested and Miss Dorsey was held for intoxication. Eventually she charged Mr. Clay with assault and battery. "That's life," Clay, Sr. said; "You know, I've never hit a woman in my whole life. But this thing cost some money. A woman starts yelling and everybody believes her. I think it's good that women should get protection, but if they yell they sure got you over the barrel."

If Clay, Jr. is known not to openly drink, smoke, or chase after women—he still refers to his father as one of the two people he is most fond of. Clay, Sr. told me: "My son has never tried to make me join no Black Muslims. He knows how I feel about it. He knows I'll never join anything that would stop me from doing what I want to do. I like girls, no matter what color their faces are. I respect anyone I think is decent. If a black man is no good, well, he's no good. If a white man is no good, the same goes for him too. To me, I judge individuals, no matter what color they are. We have good and bad in every race.

"Besides," he continued, "I like to have a few drinks once in a while."

If Cassius Clay, Jr. didn't drink and had no wife to fight with, still in his early days at Martin's gym, he made so much noise and caused so much trouble that Martin banned him from the gym. "I made him toe the line," Martin said. "I threw him out and told him I would let him back when he remembered who the boss was. When I say it's raining out, I don't want you looking out no window." Martin had a weekly boxing show on television, called "Champions of Tomorrow." The stars were the kids. Cassius received weekly television exposure and a reputation. "I knew how to match him," Martin says. "I was careful; I didn't put him in with no one I knew could beat him."

Martin recalls that Cassius was unpopular with the other boys in the Columbia Gym. "He was always bragging that he was the best fighter in the gym and that someday he was going to be champion."

In 1958, Cassius won the Louisville Golden Gloves light heavyweight crown and advanced to the quarter-finals in the Tournament of Champions in Chicago before suffering his first defeat, at the hands of Tony Madigan, who was later to meet him in a crucial bout in the 1960 Olympics.

"He was hurt in the stomach," Martin recalls, "and I signaled the referee to stop it. I didn't want the kid to get hurt unnecessarily."

A year later, a strapping six feet tall and weighing 170 pounds, Cassius, still a high school student, won the National A.A.U. light heavyweight championship at Toledo. "I am the prettiest, the greatest," he yelled, walking out to the ring. He saw me among the crowd, called me, and shouted out to the startled crowd: "Here is the prettiest middleweight in the world," raising my hand! "And I am the best-looking light heavyweight in the world." Then he asked me to walk with him to the dressing room. "People tell me that I look Spanish," he said. "We are too pretty. We *have* to become champions."

It was the beginning of a great career for Cassius Clay. And a great friendship between us. After suffering a defeat at the hands of a Marine named Johnson at the Pan American Games in Chicago in 1959, Martin's idea was to keep young Cassius in the amateurs long enough to go to the 1960 Olympic games in Rome. "Martin advised me against turning pro and trying to just fight my way up in clubs," Clay told me, "and against preliminaries, which could take years and maybe get me all beat up. He said I ought to try the Olympics and if I won, that would give me automatically a number-ten pro rating. And that's just what I did."

Cassius' father never went to see his son's performances in the ring, but he used to talk to him every time he got home. Mainly, he advised Cassius about his relationship with Martin. "You have to watch out for these cops," he said over and over again.

Clay's mother, Odessa Lee Grady Clay, had a character quite unlike her husband's: "My mother is just another sweet little fat, homey mother. She loves to stay home and cook and she goes to Baptist church every Sunday. And she doesn't meddle, don't bother nobody. She's quiet. She has light skin, a heavyset lady, and she is just as sweet as she can be. She stays home. She's always making draperies or making clothes or cooking. She don't drink, don't smoke. She's just a real picture of a good mother."

"Light skin" might have been more than a casual observation by Clay. According to Desmond Hackett of the *London Daily Express*: "The story goes that back in 1870 a splendid fellow by the name of O'Grady out of County Clare followed the old familiar trek from Ould Ireland to the new country over the water. Married a coloured woman. His son in turn married a coloured girl. One of their daughters was Odessa O'Grady." Clay's mother still signs her name Odessa Grady Clay.

She was a doting mother. When people from the neighborhood complained to Mrs. Clay about her son's bragging, she would simply say, with a trace of pride in her voice: "He started to talk at the age of ten months. And that's pretty early for a boy." Once, Mrs. Clay was coddling her baby son when he suddenly banged her in the mouth. "He loosened one of my teeth and it had to be pulled out," she told writer George Sullivan.

At the age of three he was so big he couldn't fit in his crib and had to sleep on a regular bed. And every time his mother took him on a bus, the driver made her pay for the three-year-old boy, "because he looked five."

Mrs. Clay always taught her children manners, and she kept young Clay dressed clean and wouldn't allow him to walk outside the house barefoot. Cursing was prohibited. Conventional morality was an obsession. Every Sunday she would take her children with her to church.

At the store where they used to buy groceries, the Clays never bought on credit; they always paid cash. A store clerk named Riley recalled to *Newsday*'s Bob Waters: "Mrs. Clay always paid her bills and her children were good. But that Cassius, her husband, was kinda mouthy. He was a wise know-it-all."

His father's name and his own had once belonged to that prominent Kentuckian, Cassius Marcellus Clay, who was America's Ambassador to the Court of St. James, an unsuccessful candidate for the Vice Presidency of the United States, and a Southern plantation owner. Apparently one of Muhammad Ali's forebears took the name when he was set free.

Called "The Lion of White Hall," Cassius Marcellus Clay was the leading Southern abolitionist of his time, an important enough figure to run in the famous Republican Convention in Chicago in 1860 which nominated Lincoln for President. Clay ran for the Vice Presidential nomination against Hannibal Hamlin, and received more than 100 votes on the first ballot, in fact might even have been nominated, but was considered too much of an out-and-out radical on the slavery issue.

Those were Clay's antecedents. Named after a slave owner who was a radical, he had Irish blood in his veins. It was not the most common mixture.

CHAPTER 8

As his marks went down in school (at Virginia Avenue Grade School and later at Central High), his skill as a fighter began to improve. Learning how to throw a good left hook was better than knowing about Abraham Lincoln, or the slave owner Cassius Marcellus Clay. On the other hand, Joe Martin's report cards were encouraging. "This kid has tremendous reflexes, a natural ability, a good mind for a great boxer," Martin told Clay's parents.

It was the psychological side of Clay which gave Martin a good idea of future possibilities. Fighters, no matter at what age, obtain a sort of subconscious knowledge of discipline. If a young boy goes to the gymnasium and begins to train and at the same time starts smoking, or not running in the mornings, then the boy is constructing a psychological excuse in case the actual fight goes against him. It shows an instinctive lack of self-confidence. But Clay was not that way. He wanted to be a champion, not only consciously but subconsciously.

The bragging and the emotional outbreaks that Clay showed from childhood served a double purpose. He used them to put pressure on his opponents before fights. Also, if he had any doubt about his own physical ability, this was a good way to force himself to be good.

I can also imagine Clay as a twelve-year-old who began taking punishment in the gym for carrying his dukes too low. This style created speed in his legs. With hands down one needs velocity in the legs to evade punches. To coordinate the speed of legs, one needs the speed of hands. No one can teach that. It comes naturally.

Clay always spoke about how much he used to imitate Sugar Ray Robinson's style. But what he really did was to emulate a few of Robinson's mistakes, such as pulling away from punches and punching to the body with his chin up in the air. What Clay "knew" was that he could get away with it because his opposition was, in most cases, much slower than himself. As contradictory as it may sound, those mistakes on the part of a big man like Clay made his performance more exciting, more daring, more graceful, because it seemed as if he were taking crazy chances.

No fighter ever fought entirely by the "book." But Clay created his own special blend of the classic and the insolent. As an example of his innovative thinking, take the fundamental retreat a competent trainer teaches the boxer: slide the right foot back and follow immediately with the left without crossing feet; Clay walks backward on his toes, developing his own retreat, his own rhythm, his own shuffle.

Of course, Clay's confidence in his boxing abilities was not enough. He knew he had to do something more to get people interested in coming to his fights. Even at the beginning of his amateur career, Clay searched for gimmicks to bring people to watch him. Influenced by his father's trade, Clay began reciting poems. "I told a newsman before a fight, 'This guy must be done/ I'll stop him in one.' It got in the newspaper, but it didn't catch on then." (Later, according to columnist Milton Gross, the publicist, Gary Belkin, was to write his poems for him.)

"When I started fighting seriously, I found out that grown people, the fight fans, acted like the school kids of my days," Clay said. "Almost from my first fights, I'd mouth off to anybody who would listen about what I was going to do to whoever I was going to fight. People would go out of their way to come and see, hoping I would get beat. When I was no more than a kid fighter, they would put me in bills because I was a drawing card, because I run my mouth so much. Other kids could battle and get all bloody and lose or win and didn't hardly nobody care, it seemed like, except me, maybe their families, and their buddies.

"But the minute I would come in sight, people would start hollering, 'Bash in his nose!' or, 'Button his fat lip!' or something like that. I didn't care what they said long as they kept coming to see me fight. They paid their money, they was entitled to a little fun. You would have thought I was some well-known pro, ten years older than I was."

At the end of 180 amateur fights, he had won six state Golden Gloves tournaments in Kentucky, from light to welter, and middleweight to light heavy and heavyweight divisions. As a light heavyweight he won the 1959 National Golden Gloves, and the National Amateur Athletic Union titles.

In 1960, Clay repeated his previous achievement by winning the National Golden Gloves and the National A.A.U. tournaments once more. But this time, to let his brother fight as a light heavyweight, Clay fought as a heavyweight at the A.A.U. After his brother's defeat, Clay returned to his normal weight classification at 175 pounds. At the A.A.U. championship, he gained the right to participate in the Olympic trials to be held at the Cow Palace in San Francisco. He was reaching the ultimate goal of amateur competition.

Of all the competitors at the Olympic trials, Clay was the most publicized one. He had that advantage over his opponents. He was only eighteen, but his boxing experience was notoriously unequaled by any other entrant.

When Clay walked into the ring at the Cow Palace for his second elimination fight, he was booed by many of the fans. That same day, the papers had criticized him for "boasting and bragging in a clean, pure, decent amateur tournament." For the semifinal fight, Joe Martin had to admonish Clay, threatening him with removal from the tournament if he "didn't watch his mouth." Clay reluctantly agreed to keep his mouth shut.

In the final fight of the Olympic trials, Clay faced tough Army champion Allen Hudson, a tall, slim black man with a murderous left hand. Not long ago I saw the Clay–Hudson fight film. For two rounds, Hudson held his own, making the match the toughest Clay had in the whole tournament. In the first round Clay pulling away, never saw a long, left hook which landed high on the right side of his head. Clay went down. In the second round, the fight was about even up. In danger of losing the fight, it was not until the third round that Clay, coming out of a clinch, caught Hudson with an off-balance right cross which went over Hudson's left jab to land square on the jaw. Hudson's legs gave out. Clay, taking advantage of his opponent's condition, jumped at him with a barrage that forced the referee to stop the match. Hudson, legs still weak, protested the referee's action, but too late. Clay was the light heavyweight representative of the United States Olympic Boxing Team and that would take him to Rome.

After winning the Olympic trials, he went back home for a little while to finish his last year of high school. Although he was the number one amateur light heavyweight fighter in America, he was the 367th student in a class of 391 and graduated from Central High School with a diploma inscribed "Certificate of

Attendance" given to him only because of his athletic achievements. "I was the baddest cat in Central High. Beat up all of 'em. Didn't bring no lunch to school, passed all my tests . . . 'Give me the answer or I'll hit you.' "

It was mid-summer when the United States Boxing Team was scheduled to leave for Rome. Martin was unable to accompany Clay on this trip because of an illness in his family. It was the first time that Clay would perform in a ring without Martin in his corner.

Nonetheless, Cassius Clay arrived in Rome, and began from the first day yelling, screaming, and bragging about how he was going to become the Olympic champion. His behavior brought photographers from every country and pushed other American athletes to the background. He was quickly not popular.

A teammate of Clay's, Petrol Spanakos, the U.S. bantamweight entrant, wrote: "Cassius received a $5.00 postal money order from Joe Martin in Louisville. He confided in me that he had something like a check. I told him how to endorse it and cash it. Immediately he snatched it from my hand and waved it before all the other boxers saying, 'Man, I got me a $5,000 bonus from my coach.' He received such cusses in reply that he reduced the figure to $500. Of course, he asked me not to reveal his appetite for blowing things up, an appetite he has not lost."

Clay said later: "I remember going over to the Olympics and fighting all the cats from Russia, Germany, and a fellow from Poland and Australia, living in the Olympic Village, talking to all the Mexicans, Indians, and all the people who represented various cultures. I was so popular there, they said if I run for Mayor of Olympic Village I could have won it. Wilma Rudolph was there and once I asked her to race with me. She did, and I started real good but in ten seconds she left me back so far it was a shame. I liked her a lot but I couldn't say nothing to her because a track star by the name of Ray Martin was after her. And she liked him and I wanted to beat him up one day, but I couldn't. I met all the American stars: Ralph Boston, Rafer Johnson, Don Boyd, Wilbert McClure. And we all had a great time in Rome. That was the big break, to win the World Amateur Championship."

The then heavyweight champion, Floyd Patterson, in Rome to watch the Olympics, went to see Clay. When Clay saw him among a crowd he yelled: "Floyd Patterson, some day I'm going to whup you. I am the greatest." Floyd just smiled and said, "You're a good kid, keep trying kid."

There were nineteen countries with entries in the light heavyweight division. Communist countries, which do not have "professional" fighters, entered boxers with ten to twenty years of boxing experience. As a result, their boxing experience usually surpassed that of any amateur or professional fighters in non-Communist countries.

Clay's first fight was against Belgium's Yvon Becaus, a tall, skinny boxer, who couldn't take Clay's combination punches and was finally stopped in the second round. In his second bout of the tournament, Clay faced Russian Gennadily Shatkov. It was the first time that Clay had fought a man with more experience than he had. The fight was not exciting, but Clay was able to out-jab his opponent and there was no doubt in any of the minds of the sixteen thousand at the Palazzo Dello Sport about Clay's victory or ability.

In Melbourne, Australia, in the 1956 Olympics, I fought my final fight against Hungarian Lazlo Papp, and it was not until he beat me by one point that I found out Papp had won the 1948 and 1952 Olympics, before beating me four years later. Papp had had 360 fights when he stepped into the ring to fight me, a leading U.S. amateur, who had had 28 fights.

Ali couldn't hit Shatkov with clean punches, because of the Russian's vast experience. It was his sheer ability that beat the Russian. There was a possibility that if the fight had gone over six rounds, Clay would have been in a lot of trouble. But in amateur competition you either box five two-minute or three three-minute rounds.

Beating the Russian, without a doubt, gave Clay more confidence, as he showed in his next fight against the same man he had beaten in the National Golden Gloves in Chicago a year before, Australian Tony Madigan. This time the fight was not as close. It was a hard fought battle, but Clay fought with much more intelligence than in their first encounter.

In the finals Clay drew the Polish champion, Zbigniew "Ziggy" Piertrzkowski (Ali: "Someone with 15 letters in his name"), veteran of over 230 fights. In Piertrzkowski, Clay was meeting the first southpaw he had faced since his early days as an amateur. It meant trouble—like Papp gave me. Piertrzkowski was a good southpaw, having won the bronze medal in the 1956 games, and Clay always had difficulty with the unorthodox stance of left-handers; he lost twice to them in his early days.

The fight began as a dull one. The Pole respected Clay's reputation and Clay had trouble adjusting to the awkward left-handed style of Piertrzkowski. It was not until the middle of the second round that Clay solved his rival's style and caught up with him. By the end of the round Clay took command immediately, bringing blood with two quick smashes to the face and forcing the Pole to run in an attempt to last the limit and escape the ignominy of being stopped by an American.

At the final bell, the Pole was hanging against the ropes with blood pouring from his nose, mouth, and assorted cuts around the eyes, but the record book merely shows that he lost "by decision." Martin Kane wrote in *Sports Illustrated*: "It was the bloodiest round of the Olympics. When the bell rang the Pole was all but defenseless and had been for at least the final minute."

Clay was now the best light heavyweight amateur fighter in the world—the winner of the 1960 Gold Medal.

And as far as he was concerned, Clay was the god of the Olympics, and he had proof—the gold medal hanging around his neck. "I told you! Didn't I? I am the greatest!" he began yelling all over Rome.

He took the Gold Medal to bed with him that first night and paid calls on others in the Village, telling the middleweight champion of the 1960 Olympics, Nino Benvenuti, "You're the best white fighter around."

On the day following his triumph a Russian reporter approached Ali. "How do you feel about winning the Gold Medal?" the Russian asked.

"Terrific," answered Clay.

"How does it feel to win something for a country where you can't eat at the same table with a white man?"

Clay became furious, "Tell your readers we got *qualified* people working on that and I'm not worried about the outcome. The U.S.A. is still the best country in the world."

"The man went away with nothing to write in his Russian papers," Clay said. " 'That's a bad nigger,' that Russian probably thought."

Cassius Clay flew back to America, Gold Medal hanging from a gold chain around his neck. Clay, boasting and bragging, came back to New York, instead of Louisville. Joe Martin was waiting at Idlewild Airport with good news. A Louisville businessman, a millionaire, was interested in Clay's professional career.

Martin gave Clay a tour around New York City. "I went to Greenwich Village to see the beatniks and the crazy people I heard so much about it," Clay recalls. "I went to see great Sugar Ray Robinson and I showed off around Times Square and subway stations with my Gold Medal around my neck. I also visited a store in Times Square where they make phony newspaper headlines and I had one made up that read: 'Cassius signs for Patterson.' I figured people back home wouldn't know the difference and would believe it. I spent over half an hour with Mayor Wagner. I was a very proud man. It was the biggest thing that had happened to me in my life. I was taking advantage of it."

Joe Martin had put Clay in a suite at the Waldorf which belonged to millionaire William Reynolds of R. J. Reynolds Tobacco Company. "I told him Clay could be a world champion if he got the right financial backing."

Reynolds picked up the bill, which included presents for Clay's family—watches and jewelry for his parents and brother costing over four hundred dollars. At the Waldorf, Clay ate five steaks a day, at $8.50 a steak, for four days.

After preliminary business talks, Clay and Martin went back home to Louisville.

The reception was fantastic. Among the large crowd who went to the Standiford Field Airport was Cassius Marcellus Clay, Sr. It was the first time the senior man of the family had shown interest in his son's boxing career.

The welcoming crowd was a mixed one, and he was treated as a king. "Every police car from Louisville escorted me through the streets of my town," Clay recalls. The motorcade stopped at Central High School where hundreds of students had a small program prepared for the "champ," and a huge sign reading: "Welcome home, Cassius Clay."

Clay seemed shy and modest when introduced to the crowd inside the school auditorium. "I appreciate this," Clay said. "Thank you very much."

The young kid who did crazy things to attract attention had now delivered on his promise and was being honored with one of Louisville's most effusive welcomes.

CHAPTER 9

In Louisville the deal was presented to Clay. Reynolds was to give Clay a $10,000 bonus for signing plus a guaranteed income, against earnings, for ten consecutive years. For Martin, this deal was a "favor" to Clay. The fighter would receive enough money to concentrate on boxing and not have to look for outside work. The situation is similar to being a writer who doesn't have to begin his literary work after coming home from the job.

"Billy Reynolds had watched Clay and liked him," said Martin. "He agreed with me that the boy could be champion. We had Clay and his father and Mrs. Clay and their woman lawyer, Alberta Jones, right here in the house. I thought everything was set." It wasn't.

Cassius Clay, Sr. balked. New to his son's boxing career, the elder Clay distrusted police. Martin was no exception. "He told me," Clay quoted his father, "he had made me a heavyweight by feeding me vegetables and steaks when I was a baby, and he also talked about how he had fights with my mother because she didn't want him to give me such food because I couldn't chew it. 'Son, I went without shoes for long, hard days to provide you good food and good clothes,' he told me. 'Now you should listen to me.'"

His father won. Martin said, "All of a sudden you'd think the old man did all the work. The old man never did care about what the kid was doing until Clay got all of that publicity. He's something, he is. He's got all the brains God gives a goose—about half-a-teaspoon full."

Now, recalling that time, Clay dismissed Martin in conversation, "He is an amateur man," Clay, Jr. told me. "I needed a professional man. He did a lot for me, other people did much for me, but *I* did most for *me*."

Of course, Clay's potential had not gone unnoticed outside of Louisville, either, and prospective managers flocked to his door. Cus D'Amato tried, using me as an intermediary, to interest Clay. According to writer Sullivan, Sugar Ray Robinson, as well as Pete Rademacher (the ex-Olympic Heavyweight Champion who distinguished himself by going for the Heavyweight Championship against Floyd Patterson in his first pro fight) and even Archie Moore had approached Clay. Moore handed the young fighter a card which said: "If you want a good, experienced manager, call me, collect."

Meanwhile, back in Louisville, a boxing fan who had followed Clay's amateur career with no special interest at first, but who had been greatly impressed when he won the 1959 Golden Gloves, became interested. Bill Faversham found out about the break with Martin and invited the Clays for dinner at his home. His offer was to form a syndicate of 11 men, himself included, who would give Clay a $10,000 bonus upon signing, a guarantee of $4,800 for the first two years—or $200 a month—and $6,000 as a draw against earnings, for the following four years. With his $10,000 Clay bought a year-old Cadillac for his folks and set aside $3,000 for taxes.

The contract read that the parties—Clay and the syndicate—would divide the earnings evenly, including Clay's possible extracurricular earnings outside the ring. The group of men would underwrite all travel and training expenses, including the trainer's salary, out of their half. And 15% of Clay's half was to go into a pension fund, which he could not touch until he was 35 or quit boxing.

Faversham, then the 54-year-old vice-president of a distilleries corporation in Louisville and a man whose athletic abilities were limited to freshman football and some boxing at Harvard, headed the syndicate which they called "The Louisville Sponsoring Group." As the head, Faversham would serve as the manager of record, picking the opponents, the places and the purses. The gray-haired industrialist picked, among his 10 other associates, five millionaires and most of the group was associated with, or related to, the Brown families of the Brown & Williamson Tobacco Company and the Brown–Forman Distilleries.

So Clay became the first athlete-corporation, a man to be run by a "team."

The papers signed, Clay kept calling Faversham for a fight. Finally, his first professional match was set for October 29, 1960, a month after his return from the Olympics. "First fight in Louisville, Kentucky, fought a white cat named Tunney Huntsinger from Fayetteville, West Virginia." Tunney Hunsaker, as the record book has it, was a name destined to go down in boxing history like Jack Kracken and Lee Epperson who had been the first men to fight Joe Louis and Rocky Marciano.

Bill King, the Louisville promoter, billed Clay as "The Olympic champion, turning pro in his first pro fight," and drew a big crowd, easily making his guaranteed $2,000 to Clay. The fight went the full six rounds. Clay, still wearing his Olympic trunks with "U.S.A." on the side, gained an uninspiring decision. It was not a big beginning. Former champions like Louis, Patterson, Marciano, and Frazier, won their first professional fights by knockouts. Even I knocked out my first professional opponent in the first round. You should be very keyed-up for that first professional fight. So Faversham was not impressed with Clay's performance, nor with Clay's temporary trainer, Fred Stoner of Louisville. No one had seen anything of the punching power that made Clay so exciting as an amateur. Therefore, Faversham sent his protégé to the West Coast and the boxing camp of Archie Moore. "I wanted Clay to learn some tricks from the 'old professor,'" said Faversham.

Meanwhile, Lester Malitz, who at one time had produced the Wednesday night fights on TV for Archie Foster's clients—Foster was an advertising executive and a member of the syndicate—recommended Angelo Dundee, who had been manager to Willie Pastrano and Luis Rodriguez, both champions.

Bill Faversham came down to Miami Beach and asked Dundee what he thought he could do. Dundee explained: "I would start with six-round fights until he learned. Miami will be excellent for Clay because we've got six two-minute rounds here and the changeover wouldn't be that much."

But even then Dundee knew a lot about Clay. He had first met him two years before. "I had Willie Pastrano fighting Johnny Holman in Freedom Hall in Louisville," Dundee recalls. "Willie and I were resting up in the room and watching TV and I got a call from the lobby of the hotel. The guy on the other end of the phone said, 'My name is Cassius Marcellus Clay. I won the Golden Gloves. I'm the champ of Louisville, Kentucky. I won the A.A.U. I won this tournament, I won that tournament. I want to talk to you.' So I said to Pastrano, there's some sort of a nut downstairs. He wants to talk to us. Should I tell him to come up? Willie says, 'Yeah, we got nothing better to do.'

"Up pops this good-looking big kid. He's there with his brother, Rudy. He stood there and talked to us for three and one-half hours. He told me about all the fighters I had. Who I worked with on TV. He told me I had a nickname of being a 'cut man' because I worked with Carmen Basilio. Then he asked me, 'How many miles do your fighters run?' 'Why do they run?' 'What do they eat?' 'Do they eat once a day, twice a day, three times a day?' 'What do they do prior to a fight?' 'How long do they stay away from their wives?' He wanted to know every facet of boxing! He was hungry to acquire information about boxing. See, he's a student of boxing. A lot of people don't know that. He studied boxing. I think he reads every book on boxing. He and I got to be very friendly.

"Every time I came to town with a fighter, he was there. I came to town with Ralph Dupas, Willie Pastrano three or four times, Luis Rodriguez and Joey Maxim. I was there maybe a dozen or more times and each time I got to meet him, his father and his mother.

"One night when Luis Rodriguez fought, he walked in with Luis' bag. I gave him passes to get into the fights. He and I got to be very friendly. The thing that always sticks in my mind is when I went there right after he had come back to Louisville after winning the Olympics in early 1960. He had come back and I had a fighter fighting there, as usual. And he came up to me and said, 'How come you never approached me to handle me?' And I said, 'It's this simple. You know my business is boxing. That's all I do. I have a gym in Miami Beach and if you ever want to become a fighter, come down and see me and I'll work with you.' He says: 'You've got to be some sort of a nut. Everybody approaches me, offers me all kinds of money, cars. And you, all you offer me is to come down to Miami Beach.'

" 'Certainly. What I'm offering you is what talent I have! I'm sure I can do a good job with you.' And he said: 'You've got to be some sort of a nut.' "

These two men who called each other "some sort of a nut," these men who had known large measures of success before they became associated, were then joined together, destined to form a boxing combination that would rival Kearns and Dempsey, Weill and Marciano, D'Amato and Patterson.

"Angelo Dundee," Clay told me, "I like him 'cause he's half colored. Got a lot of colored nigger blood in him. He's Italian and he passes for white, but he's got a lot of nigger in him. I get along with him. He never bosses me, tells me when to run, how much to box. I do what I want to do . . . I'm free. I go where I want to go. And he is a nice fella. Everybody likes him. He's got the connection and the complexion to get me the right protection which leads to good affection."

Dick Sadler, voted 1970's Manager of the Year by the New York Boxing Writers for his brilliant handling of 1968 Olympic Heavyweight Champion, George Foreman, told Dundee at that time: "You know, if you are able to work with this kid, you deserve a purple heart with nine clusters." Sadler had spent time with Clay and was not able to stay with him. He knew how Clay behaved.

"The whole thing was to understand him," Dundee told me.

In early December, 1960, Faversham called Dundee on the phone. "I'm going to send you the kid."

"Not yet," said Dundee. "Let him spend Christmas home." A few minutes later, Faversham called back.

"Angelo, the kid wants to fight. He wants to go *now*. He wants a fight before Christmas."

"So he came down," recalls Dundee, "by train and I picked him up in the station." Dundee drove him directly to the Smith Hotel in Miami Beach.

"It was not a good hotel," Dundee said. "But he wanted to be a fighter. So he didn't care. I got him a kid to be with him all of the time, including staying with him at the hotel. Later, after things improved Clay said to me: 'You didn't like me too much, did you? You put me in a stinkin' hotel with a guy who stunk!' The guy had body odor. A kid from the islands. He was a clean kid, but he stunk! He was from the Caribbean area. The kid stunk, but he was clean."

The smell of fighters is something. I could close my eyes in the locker room of a gymnasium and be able to tell if the man coming from the floor—after ending the workout—was black, white or Puerto Rican. It seemed as if each particular ethnic group had its own special smell. The same happened with towels left hanging on benches. Fighters were able to steal the ones which belonged to the other groups.

I remember discussing the smell of fighters with people who never had contact with gymnasiums and they used to laugh at me. And one day it occurred to me that maybe the social and economic standard of a people could have something to do with the way they smell. Different cultures have different diets; the worse the diet, the stronger the smell. Of course, sometimes you could smell a man's emotions, and if it was fear or treachery, it didn't make you too happy. Sometimes bad fighters smelled of stupidity. Maybe Clay had a fighter like that for a roommate.

Dundee had decided to put the young kid in with Clay because he didn't want his new fighter to be alone. "I hate fighters to be by themselves. They should have company to do road work," Dundee said.

"This man Clay survived every kind of situation, because he wanted to be a fighter," Dundee continued. "He used to walk from the hotel to the gym which was about five miles away."

In the gym Clay wanted to box every day and with everybody, but Angelo was the trainer. It was his job to find out when he was going to let Clay fight in the gym and with whom. "Every day he came in: 'I wanna box. I wanna box.' I said, 'Take it easy,'" Angelo recalls. "I'd only make him box with a certain kind of guy, see! But he wanted to clean up the gym. 'Let me work with him. Let me work with him.'" Dundee claims that Clay's happiest moments were in the gym. "He gets energized," Dundee says. "You know, other fighters don't. The gym is a problem. They hate to go; they hate to work. Sure, they are forced to work. So, this is the thing about Clay that makes him so great. He loves what he does."

"His ability and his natural stuff was great," Dundee recalls. "You see, I never touched the natural stuff with him. What a fighter has naturally, you can't improve on. You let it alone. You smooth it out. But you never tamper with it. All I did was improve what he had. And I added a few wrinkles. It was not the same kind of training you'd have given another fighter. In other words, you couldn't say, 'Throw a jab. Throw a left hook!' Couldn't do that. He had to be the inventor—the star."

Able to understand Clay and not minding the new technique he had to use, Dundee adjusted with no harm done to the fighter. He simply trained Clay in such a way that Clay could take credit for the improvement.

"You'd understand, José, being a fighter. Say I said, 'My gosh, you threw a tremendous uppercut, that was beautiful!' He never threw that uppercut, you see! Then, I'd say, 'Jesus, you're getting that jab down real good. You are bending your knee now and you're putting a lot of snap in it now. You knocked that guy's head back.' 'Jesus, that side-to-side movement is beautiful.' Then *he'd* do it the next round. See what I mean?"

Clay's desire to box before Christmas didn't take place. But Dundee got him a preliminary match on the undercard of the Willie Pastrano–Jesse Bowdry main event four days before New Year's.

The record shows that his opponent, Herb Siler, was T.K.O.'d in the fourth round. A newspaper description of Clay's victory went: "A right to the midsection and a left hook to the jaw. Clay walked out after his first pro K.O. saying, 'I'm gonna be the heavyweight champion of the world.'"

His next three fights took place in the same place under the promotion of Angelo's brother, Chris. Each of the fights ended early; Tony Esperti of Miami, stopped in three, February 17; Jim Robinson out in two minutes of the first round, 10 days later, a prelim to the NBA Light Heavyweight Championship Match. Donnie Fleeman got knocked out in the seventh round 14 days after the Robinson fight. It marked the first time Clay went over six rounds.

Fleeman had also been Clay's first opponent with considerable boxing experience. Holding the nice record of fifty-one fights and twenty K.O.'s among his forty-five victories, Fleeman was able to absorb Clay's punches, and could probably have gone the full eight rounds if he had not been cut so badly around both eyes that the fight was stopped in the seventh.

But one thing a young fighter learns when he begins fighting professional men with experience: they don't fall with the first good punch. An old pro has twenty different ways to shake off blows without letting his opponent know he has been hurt. Experience makes a fighter hard to hit clean in the jaw, and an old pro's best instinct is to discourage young, inexperienced fighters. Of course, Clay with his long amateur career and his ability to assimilate along with his determination had given him the ingredients to become a pro.

When Angelo took Clay back to fight in Clay's hometown, Louisville, on April 19 against the experienced farmer from Utah, Lamar Clark, Clay told the press he would knock his opponent out in two. It was his first prediction.

"Lamar Clark had a big gimmick," said Clay. "He had knocked out 45 fellows in a row. He was a white fellow with a good punch and people came to see if I could beat him."

After battering Clark to the canvas three times and breaking his nose, Clay ended it in the second round. Newsmen flew to Clay. "How did you do it?" asked a reporter.

"I just had the feeling he must fall," Clay answered with every hint that he was tuned and the elements were tuned, and they were tuned to each other. "I said he would fall in two and he did. I'll continue this approach to prove I'm great."

It would have been stupid to try to stop the workings of this new gimmick in Ali's complex mind. Even if the prediction didn't come true, there were always better reasons, or excuses or justification for failure. Clay had learned the cliché in boxing of "get off first," and "show him to respect you from the beginning." He had learned that you must work on your opponent's mind.

"From now on they all must fall in the round I call," Clay told the press. And the newsmen had a story and the young fighter had an attraction for the people and a formula for himself.

"I began predicting the outcome of my fights after watching Gorgeous George, the great wrestler. I hear this white fellow say, "I am the World's Greatest Wrestler. I cannot be defeated. I am The Greatest! I am the King. If that sucker mess up my pretty waves in my hair, I'm gonna kill him. I am the King. If that sucker whups me, I gonna get the next jet to Russia. I cannot be defeated. I am the prettiest. I am the greatest!" When he was in the ring, everybody boooooooed, boooooed. Oh, everybody just booed. And I was mad. And I looked around and I saw everybody was mad."

The glint of a suppressed laugh showed in Clay's eyes. "I saw 15,000 people coming to see this man get beat. And his talking did it. And, I said, this is a g-o-o-o-o-o-o-o-d idea!"

Next match was Kolo "Duke" Sabedong, another experienced 6'6", 226-pound journeyman from Hawaii, who had 27 fights, winning 15 of them. The fight, Clay's first ten-rounder, was scheduled for Las Vegas.

"Are you nervous about this fight?" a reporter asked.

"I'm not afraid to fight. I'm afraid of the flight."

Clay begged Dundee to go to Vegas by train. But Dundee, not looking forward to a three-day train ride, overruled him.

Clay survived the flight, but Sabedong survived Clay's fast punches, and they went ten rounds to a decision for Clay. Perhaps the flight affected Clay's reflexes because he didn't hit Sabedong with any clean punches.

More than a few champions, among them, Floyd Patterson, Ray Robinson and myself, feared airplanes. In my particular case, I was always apprehensive of flying, but when I became world's champ, my fear went from apprehension to paranoia. Becoming champion affected my behavior. My new sense of importance brought to my mind many morbid thoughts. The transition from a regular fighter to a world's champion was a deep psychological shock. From the day I won the championship until three months later, I felt strange dizziness and drunkenness that my doctor diagnosed as "mental fatigue." Said it was normal because of the emotions of the championship.

For men who believe they are strong enough to have an effect on other people, flying seems dangerous. Dangerous in the sense that they lose confidence in their ability to send the right vibrations to the pilot. And the confidence of their existence is challenged by morbid thoughts.

Unable to understand the technology of a plane, I became confused in thinking of its controls and complexities and my mind seemed forcibly channeled toward the possibility of death. I've understood that the championship had given me the consciousness of life and a great desire for it. Clay must have had similar feelings, after winning the Olympic heavyweight crown. Why not?

After Sabedong, Dundee took Clay back to Louisville and put him in with Alonzo Johnson, his first fight against a ranked heavyweight.

Johnson went the entire ten rounds with Clay, but Clay won nine out of the ten. Dundee saw something and said: "His improvement from his previous Sabedong fight was impressive. Johnson was a better fighter than Sabedong, but this time Clay boxed smart and was able to connect with clean punches. I thought he was ready for the big leagues."

Still, Dundee kept his maneuvers careful with Clay. He signed for Louisville again on October 7 against Alex Miteff. "He'll go in six," Clay announced, and in round six, banged away at Miteff until the referee was forced to stop the fight. "I am the king. I am the greatest. Nobody can stop me. They'll all fall," Clay proclaimed.

Dundee chose Willie Besmanoff as his pupil's next opponent. Besmanoff had been out of the ring for four months at that time, and Dundee figured that no matter how strong he was, he wouldn't have the timing to catch Clay. "He must fall in seven," Clay said.

"I'm embarrassed to get in the ring with this unrated duck," Clay said in a Louisville television program. "I'm ready for top contenders."

Besmanoff, a German Jew with the body of a German tank, short, stocky, powerful, was mad at Clay's remarks about him. And he showed it as soon as the bell rang for the first round. Besmanoff rushed at Clay with such anger people thought Clay was going to get massacred. But, in reality, Besmanoff was making the night tougher on himself. He became, with his madness, a perfect target for Clay's fast, accurate punches. Every time he rushed his younger and faster opponent, Besmanoff found nothing in front of him. When he turned to look for Clay, his face had gloves all over it. In round five, Besmanoff was defenseless. But Clay wanted to fulfill his prediction. So he just moved around using his jab, while Dundee yelled at him: "Stop playing around. Stop playing around."

The beginning of round seven showed a different fighter. Clay came up with an aggressive attitude not shown in the previous rounds. He stalked his opponent and hit him with fast, strong jabs and followed those with straight right-hand punches. His last punch was a straight right to the jaw. Besmanoff went back, down and out. Nothing moved in his body for over ten seconds. It was a display of punching power, and of accuracy and speed while delivering the punches. "When he was not playing around, he looked like a champ," remembered Dundee.

Everyone, including Clay, was impressed with this fight. New York became his next stop. The "Big Leagues" were approaching.

CHAPTER 10

You go to New York for the same reason Willie Sutton robbed banks: that's where the money is.

For pugilists New York means Madison Square Garden. Many kids become fighters with the idea that one day they will be standing in the ring of the Garden, while a man in a tuxedo calls their names to the world.

Yet, in the richest city of the world, Madison Square Garden pays its preliminary fighters today what it paid them 30 years ago—$150 for four rounds, $500 for six rounds, $1,500 for eight rounds (except for rare occasions). As far as four, six and eight-rounders who perform in the Garden are concerned, their fees have stood still while every other sport has increased payments to its athletes. But fighters, most of them, don't even really care about the money, in fact, they don't even know they are being underpaid; they simply want to appear in Madison Square Garden, and will fight for nothing if necessary. Small-time managers are also excited by the place.

To Angelo Dundee, however, the Garden was familiar, as were its liabilities, and when he made his decision to let Clay come to New York, he was not about to rush him into there. But when a heavyweight fight between two of the top contenders was cancelled just five days before their scheduled bout, Dundee accepted a match he thought was "right." The opponent was young Sonny Banks, an up-and-coming fighter who was building his own record and following in and around Detroit.

For by February 1962, the young Olympic light heavyweight champion had become the most interesting sports news in the local papers. Taking advantage of newsmen's predicted attitudes, Clay again began predicting victory.

"The man must fall in the round I call," said Clay. People laughed. "In fact," Clay continued, "Banks must fall in four."

The first round began with Clay dancing around with his hands down. Banks, known for his good, fast, hard left hooks, kept missing his favorite punch. Clay smiled, and danced around his opponent some more. This pattern continued through early rounds. Then, unexpectedly, a long left hook in the third caught Clay on the jaw. He went to the floor and the crowd went to its feet. When Clay got up, Banks charged. Clay concentrated on defense and got through the round. In the fourth, Clay came out fast. Before the round was over, Banks was out and Clay, his mouth open again said, "I told you. The man fell in four."

Clay had won again in the round he had predicted. But Dundee, after seeing his fighter on the floor, decided not even to stay in New York. Still, Clay had left his mark, and must have missed New York. John F. X. Condon, the publicist for Madison Square Garden, remembers: "When Clay first came here, he was he same as he is now. Same type of a personality. He cried for attention. He used to stand, in the days of the old Garden, on the corner of 49th and Broadway, just to see how many people would recognize him!"

Dundee, however, had brought Clay back to Miami and chose Don Wagner as Clay's next opponent. The fight was scheduled for the Miami Beach Auditorium for February 28, just two and a half weeks after the Banks fight. Because Wagner had about as much experience as Banks, Clay said: "Wagner must fall in four. He should not go longer than Banks." The fight wasn't too tough for Clay. He could have taken Wagner earlier, but carried him, then knocked him out in the predicted fourth round. This was a pattern he had repeated time and again, letting his opponent remain alive until the right round had come up.

Dundee next took Clay to Los Angeles to fight George Logan, "A real pro, with a lot of experience and a good puncher," Dundee characterized him. Logan was also known as a terrific left-hooker. This time Clay, consistently, made Logan's hooks look silly. The improvement in Clay was impressive and Dundee felt that his fighter was now ready for tougher opposition.

Billy Daniels, a tall, light-skinned black from New York was also considered promising by the press. Dundee brought his fighter back to New York but not for Madison Square Garden; once again, to St. Nicks.

In a hard, and awkward, fight of holdings, clinches and pushes, Clay finally stopped Daniels on cuts in round seven. Despite this unimpressive showing, Archie Moore came next. This was Clay's first big test. "The decision was made in minutes," recalls Dundee, "and when we told Clay, he got excited."

His standard as a fighter would be elevated to that level where he could never come back to face inferior opposition. It was an advance from which there was no return. If he failed, well, maybe he was one more fighter and not made of championship material.

West Coast promoter Ailene Eaton scheduled the Clay–Moore fight for October 23, 1962. The publicity began building up, but two weeks before the fight Eaton discovered that sales at both the closed-circuit outlets and the arena were far below the break-even point. So, hoping for Moore and Clay to insult each other a little more and thereby help ticket sales, Eaton pushed the fight back.

"You mean another three weeks of listening to him shoot his mouth off?" Moore complained to Mrs. Eaton. "That's good because I'm going to develop the 'lip-buttoner punch,' especially designed for that fresh boy." In rebuttal, Clay came up with a poem:

> Archie had been living off the fat of the land
> I'm here to give him his pension plan.
> When you come to the fight don't block aisle or door,
> 'Cause ya all going home after round four.

Adding: "If I tag him earlier, I'll just have to hold him until the fourth round." Seeing his chances to fight for the heavyweight crown (and also publicity) Clay boasted: "Just as soon as I annihilate the old man (Moore), I'll rush over to Liston and tell him he's next."

When Moore walked into the ring, his head was covered with gray hair. It was his twenty-fifth year as a professional boxer and although he admitted to be forty-three, many people thought he was forty-three, going on fifty. No longer able to make the light heavyweight limit, Moore held his aging paunch in with an elastic support pair of trunks that almost came up to his nipples.

Clay used his left jab and long, not-too-hard left hooks in the first round with Moore chasing slowly after him. In the second, with Moore still following him all around the ring, Clay moved fast and with caution without throwing too many punches. At the end of the round, Moore caught Clay with a sneaky right hand near the jaw that had the crowd cheering. In the third round Clay came out throwing lefts and rights which seemed to make Moore retreat in panic. "I could feel him getting tired," Clay said. Clay slowed up, looking for the right spots in an attempt to discourage his older opponent.

In the fateful fourth round, Clay rushed toward the tired Moore and began throwing fast combinations, knocking the "old professor" down for the automatic eight count. When Moore got up, it was just a matter of time before Clay would put him down and out. But the referee didn't wait. When Clay began raining another series of combinations on the now helpless Moore, the referee stepped between both fighters to prevent Moore from taking further punishment, and raised Clay's hand proclaiming him the winner of the fight, and effectively ending Moore's long and hard career as a fighter.

The fight had been seen all over the United States on closed-circuit TV, and that was something which hadn't been done for a non-championship fight since "Irish" Bob Murphy and Jake LaMotta squared off in a tough over-the-weight match some 12 years earlier.

Among the New York viewers were Harry Markson and Teddy Brenner, the boxing promoter and matchmaker, respectively, of Madison Square Garden. Feeling that Clay had demonstrated both his pulling power and his punching power, and that Patterson's drawing power was somewhat tarnished by his loss of the title to Liston the previous September, Markson said: "I know Patterson has a return bout contract with Liston, but I'm sure Floyd realizes that because of his one-round knockout by Liston, there will be little interest in their return unless he does *something* to restore public confidence in his fighting ability." That "something" was Clay. Of course, Patterson, assured of another chance to regain his lost crown, rejected the idea.

Clay with his eyes on the championship would have turned down the offer, too. Clay had looked so good in knocking out Moore that both Faversham and Dundee felt that their fighter was now ready to fight for the championship.

The campaign began and Clay was invited on national television shows. The press began taking the young "braggart" seriously, but still not seeing Clay as great as he proclaimed himself to be. For the moment he had brought boxing back to life. Many reporters were anxious to see Clay in the same ring with Liston just to see Liston demolish the "Louisville Lip."

While the campaign was going on, Dundee felt it would hurt his fighter to keep him inactive. Nor did he want to take matches in which his fighter could lose the chance to fight Liston or the winner of the Liston–Patterson return match. A fighter always wants to fight good fighters; a manager wants the money. So, Dundee got ex-'49ers star defensive lineman Charley Powell in Pittsburgh in January of 1963, and as per prediction, Clay took out Powell in the third round.

Meanwhile, there were noises that the World Boxing Association was going to take Liston's title away if he went through with his announced return match with Patterson, for the W.B.A. did not recognize return-bout clauses. The threats gave Clay some hope he might be in line for a crown. But the rumors quieted down, the Liston–Patterson match was sanctioned by every boxing organization in the world, including the "flexible" W.B.A., and Clay was relegated to being just another "ranking" heavyweight.

Faversham and Dundee decided to bring Clay back to New York. Doug Jones, a top contender for the light heavyweight championship, who was now campaigning as a heavyweight, had acquired the number two spot in the ratings. Dundee, the only man who really knew boxing in Clay's camp, thought Jones wouldn't offer his contender any trouble and signed for the fight to be held in March of 1963.

Publicity for the fight was reduced to radio and television because of a 95-day-old New York newspaper strike.

"This is unfair to the many boxing fans New York City has. Now they won't be able to read about the great Cassius Clay," said Cassius Clay.

But the fight was not affected by the newspaper strike. A week before the fight, there were no tickets available. In fact, the promotion gained more by exposing Clay before the TV cameras. He built the fight into such an attraction that for the first time in thirteen years the Garden at 50th Street was sold out. On every radio or TV show, Clay came up with his prediction, pugilistic and poetic:

> Jones likes to mix.
> So I'll let it go six.
> If he talks jive,
> I'll cut it to five.
> And if he talks some more,
> I'll cut it to four.

The day before the fight, Bob Waters visited Clay in his room at the Hotel Americana. "It's all this running around that gets me," he told Waters. "Last week or so it's been: 'Cassius will you be on my TV show?' 'Cassius, will you cut a tape for radio?' 'Cassius, will you pose for pictures?' Man, I'm tired. And all the time I gotta talk, you know. People expect it. Reporters say, 'We don't want to ask you questions, man. Just talk.' My mouth is tired."

Waters wrote that Clay's tired mouth had almost a minute's rest, when he suddenly sat up.

Bobby Nelson, a friend of Clay's, had just come in. He wanted Clay to meet a man named Drew Bundini Brown. "They *both* love to talk," Bobby said. "They look like they could get along pretty good."

"He (Clay) was setting back like a young little king," Bundini recalls, "with his arms spread across the couch. Just setting there.

And he began talkin' to me. But he had more in his mind than I knew. I guess he was giving me a test or something and I didn't know it. Anyway, he got down to the meat," Bundini recalled. "He asked me what kind of fighter did I think he was. I told him I thought he was a phony and he looked at me and said: 'Why you say that?' I told him: 'Because nobody in sports ever called the round on nobody.' And if we had kept it up the way we was talking, we wouldn't be together today. But the kid poured it on me. He said: 'Well, I call the round, I go there to do the best I can, and they fall.' Then, he started looking a little different to me, 'cause when a person say they do the best they can and they get results, I have no complaints. I was indeed impressed by then the first time with him.

"What you see and what you read and what you meet is three different things. That's why Indians say 'you must walk in man's moccasins for ten days, before you can talk about him.' You always give people a chance."

"My man, you're ok," Bundini quoted Clay as saying. "I've been traveling all over the world but you are the man I would like to see with me." Bundini said he simply smiled because, as he put it, "I didn't know what I could do for him."

Bundini is a striking looking man with a conspicuous long scar which goes down his right cheek. As a man in the boxing game put it, "put a headdress and beads on him and you have a witch doctor." George Plimpton described him, "a strangely gentle man in the midst of all that violence."

When I first met Bundini, I found myself hesitant to talk to him. His eyes searched mine and for over a minute he just stared at me. Then he said, "You are a great fighter. Maybe one day you could fight against Clay and make a lot of money."

He looked to me like a man who would shoot you without a minute's notice. But after you spend time with him, you can find softness beneath his hypnotizing eyes.

"Later, the same night at Bobby Nelson's home," Bundini said, "we were coming down in the elevator and Clay said to me, 'How many tickets would you like to have?' I said, 'Tickets, man, the place is sold out to the roof. People coming from all over the world. Even the crows and the pigeons have to get out of the Garden to give up seats.' " Clay just laughed.

The following day when Bundini went to his hotel room to get the tickets, "Clay was laying in this bed with the sheet up all over him."

According to Bundini, Clay got excited when he saw his "new friend" in his room. "He went and told Angelo Dundee," Bundini recalls, " 'Guess who's over here, guess who's over here? Bodini, Bo-dini.' I didn't know Angelo and he didn't know me. Me and Clay started walking around making a lot of noise, hollering and talking about the spacemen and people and stuff. We were a lot alike. More alike than anybody I ever met in my life." And, in fact, they look close enough in feature to be in the same family.

Bundini's first realization that he could find a place for himself in Clay's camp occurred late that afternoon in Clay's hotel room.

"There was a big, big man sitting in a corner," Bundini remembers, "smoking a cigar. And I seen his (Clay's) boxing gear all laid out. It was real dirty and his shoes were dirty. So being a friend, I knew he'd accepted me, I asked him, 'Who takes care of you?' He pointed to this guy. I said, 'Why don't you fellows clean his shoes up? The whole world is watching this young man. Get some polish that won't be rubbing off on his legs when he be moving around, and clean his shoes. Wash his shoestrings.' "

At that moment the telephone rang and Clay picked it up. "It was Nat King Cole," Bundini recollects, "who was calling for a pair of tickets. 'It's the great Nat Cole,' Clay whispered to those present. 'He wants tickets for the fight, but it's going to be hard to find tickets for him.' At that moment I interjected, 'You can't turn him down,' I said. 'Nat is a special kind of person. Now what you have to do is call Teddy Bremmer (Madison Square Garden's matchmaker) and if he has no tickets, tell him to put two folding seats down on the floor.' Clay agreed to do just that."

When the limousine came to pick Clay up to report to the Garden that night, Bundini found himself right in there with Clay. "We went up to the 49th Street side and I told the chauffeur to stop at the door that my fighter goes in. Then some police officer came over and said we couldn't stop there. I said, 'Stop the car. Let me speak to him.' I got out and I said to him, 'This is Cassius Clay.' He said, 'I don't care who he is, he can't stop here.' I said, 'Well, if it wasn't for Cassius Clay, you wouldn't be out here directing traffic.'

" 'I have nothing to do with it,' the cop said. 'I'm only taking orders.' "

"Let me talk to your superior," Bundini said. Finally they were allowed to park the car right at the entrance of the 49th Street side of the Garden, the fighters' entrance.

"The Champ (Bundini claims that he had always called Clay 'the Champ' since he first met him) said again that he needed me," Bundini said. "Then Clay smiled."

Coming in at about 7:30 just a few hours before the actual fight, Clay saw a group of kids waiting for his autograph. Clay told the special guard to let the kids in for a few minutes. Then signaling them to follow him, Clay stepped inside the ring and began shadowboxing while the children applauded hysterically. Some of the people who had started to come into the Garden couldn't believe that the man moving around the ring was Cassius Clay, the star of the real show at 10:00 P.M.

After this "special show" the kids left the Garden and Clay went straight to his dressing room. Bundini stepped in with Clay. He was asked to leave. Not being one of the official trainers he was not allowed to be in the room with Clay. "I'm not getting out," Bundini said. "Anyway, I'm in here with the Champ." Clay simply smiled and looked at him. "The only reason I'll go is when Clay tells me to go, because I'm his guest. I'm not in here because of you fellows." Clay then asked Bundini to wait outside. Bundini walked out and waited on the steps in the hall where Clay would have to walk through to go to the ring.

"I waited right there and when the 'Champ' came out, I grabbed him on the back and walked to the ring with him. I rubbed his back all the way down. He had 'Cassius Clay' written on his robe." Of course, Bundini was not a licensed trainer and couldn't be in Clay's corner.

Doug Jones, looking like an overstuffed light heavyweight, was the first man to enter the ring. He had weighed 188 pounds for the fight. Clay was 203.

Two weeks before the fight the odds had Clay 4–1 favored. But by the moment they stepped into the ring, odds had dropped to 2–1, with Clay still the man to beat.

"How tall are you?" Clay asked Doug while they were both in the ring, before being introduced to the fans. "Why do you want to know?" retorted Jones. "So I'll know how far to step back when I knock you out in the fourth." And Cassius just kept moving around the ring with a broad smile on his face.

When Clay walked toward Jones after the initial bell in the first round, his moves resembled the grace of a ballet dancer. Doug Jones started chasing his faster opponent. After about two minutes of the first round, Jones caught Clay against the ropes with a right cross to the jaw and Clay's legs looked weak. The crowd stood up; Clay was in trouble. Jones kept trying for an early knockout in that first round, but Clay was able to take Jones' punches and at the end of the first round, Clay had apparently recovered.

For the next three rounds Clay was still having trouble connecting with good punches even though his jabs were doing marvels for him. Every time he was tagged, Clay came right back with jabs.

It seemed as if Clay was more concerned about making Jones miss his barrage of punches than in establishing his own attack.

At the end of the fourth round Clay looked more confident. He had found his range. Just before the bell ended this round, Clay had Jones against the ropes hitting him at will. But, with ten seconds to go in the fourth round, he was unable to carry out his prediction. The people began booing.

By 1963, Cassius Clay had conditioned the boxing fans to expect exactly what he guaranteed them—a knockout in a predicted round. Right twelve times already, it was the failure of his fourteenth K.O. prediction that created almost as much excitement as a knockout.

When Clay came back after the eighth round, Angelo Dundee told him that if he didn't win the last two rounds, he was going to blow the fight, and Clay came out like a tiger in rounds nine and ten, yet never came close to flooring Jones.

There was a lot of expectation when announcer Johnnie Addie picked up the microphone to announce the decision.

Wearing a tuxedo with a bow tie, Addie began: "Judge Frank Forbes and Judge Artie Aidala, both score the fight five rounds for Clay, four rounds for Jones and one even."

The capacity crowd of 18,732—first capacity crowd for the "old" Garden in a non-championship fight since middleweight Jake LaMotta beat Italy's Tiberio Mitri back on July 12, 1950—started booing and yelling "fake."

In the noise, no one could hear the referee's score of eight rounds for Clay, one for Jones and one even. Many others had Jones winning. The Associated Press scored it 5–4–1 for Jones.

Now, standing in the middle of the ring and listening to the dissatisfied "boos" for the first time in his life wasn't enough for Clay. He had to dodge crumbled cups, cigars, flying programs and other missiles as he hurriedly left the ring.

When Jones stepped out of the ring, he was received with no ovation from the disappointed crowd.

"Doug Jones was one of the toughest fights I had," Clay stated in the post-fight press conference.

Someone said, "Clay almost didn't have the yen to finish the entire ten."

Dundee, on the way back to the dressing room, provided Clay with his excuse, "Well, you told them first that 'Jones likes to mix, and you'll let it go six,' and then you said, 'cut it to four,' so four and six make ten, see?" Clay saw and offered it to reporters as his rationale for missing his prediction.

Meanwhile, Bundini Brown, an attentive observer, was satisfied with Clay's performance. "Doug Jones hit Clay with a right hand that no guy in the world had ever hit him with. If it wasn't for the ropes he would have went down," he said. "Besides, my man here punched both to the body and to the head, and I was told that he had never punched to the body before. This man is ready to fight the champ. He's ready."

Offers poured into them. First and foremost were the demands that he give Doug Jones a chance to avenge his unpopular loss. Then the Garden started working for a match with deposed heavyweight champion Ingemar Johannson. Finally, there was a tour of Europe, put together by English promoter Jack Solomon, to show off Clay to the curious Europeans.

It was decided by the Louisville Brain-Trust that Clay should go to England to fight European Champion Henry Cooper, who was old, slow, well-ranked and, therefore, the perfect match.

While the 29-year-old Englishman had a reputation of hitting only once to win fights, and everyone described him as "the man with the best left hook in the business," he also had the reputation of starting to bleed if you happened to take a hard look at his face.

Clay's name had already reached England. In London he hit it off big. In a negative way. He said: "I'm only here to mark time before I annihilate that big ugly bear (Sonny Liston)"; described Buckingham Palace as "a swell pad"; called Cooper "a tramp, a bum and a cripple, not worth training for," and vowed: "I'll take him in five."

Previously he had said that " 'Enery (as Cooper was affectionately called) would go in two." "Or maybe one." When a reporter asked him about the discrepancy, Clay said, "I want to give the fans their money's worth."

"Henry Cooper," he said, "will think he's Gordon Cooper (the American astronaut) when I put him in orbit."

Cooper himself wasn't saying much. "I came to meet him," he said, "but all I've done is hear him."

"Can't you get that Cooper to say something? Is he that scared?" Clay said in a B.B.C. television interview.

"Surely, by now, Clay knows that everybody in Britain, including me, hates his guts," commented Cooper.

At the British Boxing Board of Control, Clay was informed that the referee would be the sole judge. "It's the greatest system in the world," Clay crowed. "But I'm gonna make the referee's job easy by kayoing Cooper." Clay kept telling the newsmen that he was not training hard for "this bum" but Dundee gave him the lie. "Clay is as fit as is humanly possible," Angelo said. "He has done miles of road work in Hyde Park and has boxed 96 rounds with his brother Rudolph and (Jimmy) Ellis."

June 18, 1963, was a beautiful day in London. Jack Solomon was announcing on radio that there were no more tickets for sale. Once again Clay was making history for the promoters. By now,

hours before the fight, assured of a sellout, Clay was only talking about his inevitable fight against champion Sonny Liston.
"I'm the greatest," he shouted. "I can draw them in no matter
who I'm with. But there wouldn't be no fight unless I get my cut.
They have been paying the challengers nothing. I've talked up the
greatest fight in history. Man, I don't need Liston. He needs ME."
Cooper, if one is to believe in Clay's promotional gifts, was irrel-
evant for his "upcoming fight with Liston."

"If Cooper whups me, I'll get down on my hands and knees,
crawl across the ring and kiss his feet. And then I'll take the next
jet out of that country, whichever country it happens to be, and
I will be wearing a false mustache and beard." (Obviously referring to Floyd Patterson's disguise after his loss to Liston.)

By fight time the odds hardened to 4–1, Clay. Six historically-
clad trumpeters blasted away as Clay, 207, and Cooper, 185½,
strode toward the ring. It was Clay's 19th fight and he was wearing a white-trimmed scarlet bathrobe with the words "Cassius
the Greatest" inscribed on the back. Cooper came in looking
nervous and well aware that his 27–8–1 record carried five losses
by knockouts and three of them by cuts.

The first round began with Cooper charging Clay, throwing
punches from every angle. Normally a slow starter, the British
champion surprised everyone and the fans were standing up giving their fighter an ovation. At the end of the round, after being
chased by his lighter opponent, Clay walked to his corner with a
bloody nose.

But the second round began with Clay using his best weapon,
his left jab. A minute later there was a little cut over Cooper's
left brow. The cut was widened in the third as Clay whipped over
four solid left jabs. Then Clay threw combination punches and
thought he had found the range. Then, he just toyed with his foe,
as if to make him last until the fifth, his predicted round.

His vanity almost cost him the fight. After two minutes of fight in the fourth round, bleeding from cuts under and over the eyes, Cooper followed Clay until the "Louisville Lip" was against the ropes, and Cooper let go with one of his famous long, wild left hooks landing it flush on Clay's jaw. Clay railed back and down with his arms tangled in the second rope. Everybody in the stadium was up as the bell rang with Clay still trying to stand. But as Cooper walked back to his corner, blood was covering his entire face.

Cassius was helped to his stool. He was probably ready to recover in the sixty-second rest period, but trainer Angelo Dundee had a different idea. One of Clay's gloves had some padding sticking out, not much, but visible to the professional eye of Dundee who promptly tore open the glove to expose nearly all of the padding. He was thereby able to demand a new pair while Clay worked to regain his focus. So the rest period between rounds four and five stretched out at least one minute longer and Clay, with a clear head, began the fifth round by swarming all over his foe.

The fans, who in round four had begged the referee to stop the fight, began chanting again: "Stop it! Stop it!" and threw missiles into the ring. Screaming among the wild crowd were Elizabeth Taylor and her husband Richard Burton. Two hard jabs snapped Cooper's head back and referee Tommy Little stepped in to stop the match. Cooper, nearly blinded and smeared with a ghastly red over both eyes, didn't argue with the decision. Turning to the referee, Cooper said, "We didn't do too bad for a 'bum and a cripple,' did we?" Adding, "If both my eyes were not closed in the fourth round, I would have knocked him out."

"Cooper shook me up," Clay admitted. "He hit me harder than I've ever been hit. Cooper is a real fighter."

Jack Nilon, Liston's advisor who was in London to see the Clay–Cooper fight, went to Clay's dressing room. "I'll demolish Sonny in eight rounds," Clay yelled at Nilon, "and he'll be in a worser fix if I predict six."

Nilon gave Clay a mock dirty look, but before he had a chance to open his mouth, Clay spoke again. "I'll fight Liston—if the price is right," Clay said. Nilon quickly assured him: "You can have the fight, kid, and the price will be right."

It seemed as if the only thing that could prevent a Liston–Clay match was if Liston was defeated in his impending match against Floyd Patterson.

"If Telstar is working," Clay predicted, "a Clay–Liston fight would draw a hundred-million-dollar gate. I'm very big in those foreign countries. They love me over there."

CHAPTER 11

Written across the top of the bus was, "World's Most Colorful Fighter," under that "Liston must go in 8." It was about three A.M. when driver Cassius Clay made an unscheduled stop in Denver, Colorado. "We decided to pay Liston a visit," said Clay. "And we started yelling: 'oink, oink!' Everybody heard. You know how them white people felt about that black man (Liston) who had just moved in. We didn't help it much. Liston came out after the taunting, but before he could make up his mind what to do, the police came and told us to leave or we'd be arrested for disturbing the peace." Clay just continued his ride, which had commenced in Los Angeles, to New York. But the "unexpected" stop in Denver was not entirely out of Clay's plans when he left the West Coast.

This had been the closest Clay had come to Liston. "It was the first time I needled him directly." Clay must have heard about Budd Schulberg's "The Harder They Fall" in which Toro Molino moved from town to town in a similar bus, campaigning for his fights. It was Clay's latest gimmick. But Cassius was not about to end his effort in persuading the boxing promoters all over the country that he was the man who could bring in the most money in a heavyweight championship match. Of course, Clay, in the mind of most of the so-called experts, had *no* chance to win the fight.

Clay was only twenty-one and had only nineteen fights when he announced that he was ready for Liston. Former undefeated heavyweight king Rocky Marciano, 40, thought that Clay was crazy. "The Lip," Marciano said, "should see either a good psychiatrist or a good tax man. I certainly don't consider Clay's decision to fight Sonny Liston very smart, for a lot of reasons."

Marciano went on to explain why Clay was crazy. "First," he said, "he's horribly short of experience to be going against a brute like Liston. Clay may have the basic tools but he's at least a year away from full maturity, both physically and as a strategist. Second, he'd better start checking with some accountants if he thinks he's going to take home any fortune even from a lollapalooza of a fight like this one. What can he keep? Ten percent? Maybe. And it takes more than that to make up for a busted head." Then the man who never lost a fight during his professional career tried to give another justification for his views.

"I had Al Weill handling me and he was as smart as they come about really educating a fighter.

"When I started I had eleven straight K.O.'s inside three rounds, fighting mostly around Providence. Then they took me into Philadelphia and I fought Gilley Ferron, and I knocked him out in three rounds, but Al and Charley Goldman, my trainer, saw some things I was doing wrong, so it was back to school for me.

"It wasn't until I beat Rex Layne in 1951 in my 36th fight that they really thought I knew what I was doing. Then I was like Clay is now—the talk of the town."

But Marciano contended that there was a difference. "I'd done all my studying," he said, "and Clay hasn't done much.

"I guess it's quite hard to tell Clay not to fight this monster now," Marciano continued, "but I'm sure he'll be more receptive after he's been there with Liston."

Joe Louis, who lends himself to be used by boxing promoters, was quoted as saying that Clay would last longer than Floyd Patterson had with Liston. That is: he would last over two minutes and six seconds.

Sonny Liston had become an instant "killer." The way he had disposed of Patterson was so impressive that writers all over America labeled him "the invincible one," or "the man who'll be there as long as he wants."

Liston, who had been training hard for his return bout with Patterson, was anxious to fight Clay. "That fag wouldn't last a round," he said, referring to Clay. "He wouldn't be there longer than Floyd."

On the night of July 22, 1963, Sonny Liston and Floyd Patterson put Las Vegas into the boxing history books. It was the first time a heavyweight championship match was going to take place there. But the fans didn't enjoy the history-making event for long.

One hundred and thirty seconds after the sound of the bell for the commencement of the first round, we all witnessed its sudden ending. Patterson had succumbed for the second consecutive time, under the powerful punches of Liston. Both fights had ended in the first round. Both almost to the exact second. This time the fight had gone 2:10 minutes.

The following day newsmen all over the country wrote about how invincible Liston was. Few thought that Clay had a chance with Sonny.

Forty-three of the forty-six sportswriters in this country predicted that they couldn't see Clay walking out of the ring. Of course, many people saw in a Clay–Liston match a chance for Clay's mouth to be finally closed. Clay had created a negative motivation for the fans. People would come not to see Liston's victory but Clay's defeat. Clay was aware of this and kept shooting off his mouth.

The bragging forced Sonny to talk. "If they ever make the fight," Liston said, "I'll be locked up for murder."

Politicians of course couldn't be kept out of the picture. California's Governor Edmund G. Brown didn't like boxing and he wanted it abolished. But his appointee, Attorney Sol Silverman, who had become a boxing investigator after former world's featherweight champion Davey Moore died of injuries sustained in a fight against Sugar Ramos not long before the intended Liston–Clay fight cried out: "Such mismatches not only endanger the overmatched boxer, but degrade boxing from a great sport to a sordid racket . . . let it be remembered that professional boxing at this time can't stand another disaster. The proposed Cassius Clay–Sonny Liston heavyweight title fight is a dangerous mismatch which could result in grave injury to the young challenger. Besides," Silverman continued, "not one former heavyweight champion among the eleven now living regards Clay as being ready for Liston."

To add to the difficulties, Clay in November of 1963 was ready to be called up for military service. Another obstacle to the match. Faversham was using all his influence to convince the Army not to induct his fighter before his match with Liston. "We don't want Clay to have something he is not entitled to," Faversham said. "But we feel this is an extenuating circumstance. If his entry into the service were delayed a few months it would give him his big chance."

Liston found out about the efforts being made to prevent Clay from going into the military service. "Well," he said, "I think I can help on this matter. You put him into the ring with me before the Army gets him and you can bet any amount of money that the Army wouldn't want 'pretty boy' after I finish him off. I'll do him a big favor."

Meanwhile, Chris Dundee, Miami boxing promoter and brother of Angelo, was pulling strings in Florida to bring the fight there. Liston, who was living in Philadelphia at the time, was also trying his best to set the proposed match in the city where old-time great Philadelphia Jim O'Brien won the light heavyweight crown . . . with Liston as the promoter.

In boxing the champion has the power. Especially when no promoter can control him. In Liston's case, he was often accused of dealing with gangsters, and promoters were careful in dealing with him. But Clay was also playing a role in the making of this match. For Clay was hardly a typical challenger. He, rather than the champ, had the drawing power. Experts had speculated that a Liston–Clay fight would bring no less than eight million dollars—a figure unheard of, even in heavyweight boxing. Working on the mechanics of the fight, Liston's people, especially Jack Nilon, the concessionaire who was running the business for the champion, could not force the fight on Clay's people. "If the money is not right," Faversham said, "my boy will not fight. He is still young, getting stronger and better. We can wait. Liston won't be there forever."

Liston had to bend a little. To make the kind of money a Liston–Clay match would draw, Liston would have had to fight at least three times. The magic words for Nilon were "easy fight," and "lots of money." Still, who knows what the psychological effect was on Liston to recognize that he was not the draw?

In August 1963, Clay went on TV in Louisville to announce that the Liston–Clay match was off. "I had talked too much and worked too hard to take a low financial cut so, since I built it up,

I'll tear it down," he said. "There will be no fight between Liston and I until the money is right.

"I'm the talk of the world. I am known as the predictor. The 'Big Bear' needs me. So if I have to take low, I had just rather not fight." Clay sounded serious. It was up to Liston's people to make the next move. Either more money or no fight.

"He either meets my price or he can dance elsewhere for peanuts," Clay continued. "I don't need Sonny Liston. He needs *me*.

"I'm the hottest attraction to come along since talking pictures. Pick up any magazine, there's Cassius Clay on the cover. I'm not talking about boxing magazines. Anybody can get in those. I'm talking about the magazines that reach the non-fight fan. When you interest that type of person you've got it made. That's where the real money is."

On November 5, 1963, Sonny Liston and Cassius met in a room at Denver's Brown Palace Hotel to sign for their world's heavyweight championship fight.

No site had yet been chosen and before bargaining was done Los Angeles, Las Vegas, Atlantic City, Minneapolis, and Chicago put in their bids. Miami Beach was to get it and the event would take place at the Convention Hall on February 25.

"I'm not afraid of Liston," Clay said after questions from the press. "He's an old man. I'll give him talking lessons and boxing lessons. What he needs most is falling down lessons." There was no reason for Clay to keep up his bragging if it were really true that he had only done it to make the Liston match a possibility. But papers signed, Clay continued with his name-calling strategy.

It was neither an accident nor an outrageous tactic. Keeping his mouth big helped to sell the match, kept the heat on Sonny Liston's psyche, and helped to convince himself that he could beat "The Bear."

On the morning of February 25, when all the training was over, when the rhetoric was supposed to be forgotten, when the war of nerves at the weigh-in would commence, Cassius Clay went "crazy."

Wearing a blue denim work jacket with "Bear Hunting" written in red script across the back, Clay thundered into the Cypress Room in Convention Hall to shock hundreds of reporters who had assembled. They had not come unprepared for Clay's antics but the expected show had increased its ante and become unexpected.

Flanked by Sugar Ray Robinson and Bundini, Clay rushed through the hundreds of newsmen without taking a second to stop. His eyes seemed to be searching for Liston. "You can tell Sonny I'm here with Sugar Ray," he screamed.

"Liston is flat-footed, but me and Sugar Ray are two pretty dancers." Adding: "Round eight to prove I'm great." He turned to Bundini and they both chanted their "Float like a butterfly, sting like a bee" routine at the top of their lungs.

When he was asked to step onto the platform where the scale was, special cops wouldn't let Sugar Ray or Bundini up with him. Now wearing white boxing trunks with black stripes and a terrycloth robe, Clay refused to climb up to the platform. "Let 'em up," he yelled. "This is my show, this is my show." Sugar Ray signaled that he didn't care, but Bundini tried to persuade the special cops. "I'll keep him quiet," Bundini said. "I have to be up there to keep him quiet." The cops waved all three up.

Moments later Liston and his entourage silently entered the room to deafening applause. Sugar Ray and Bundini tried in vain to keep Clay from jumping up and down and pretending he was going to charge the champ.

Clay's pulse rate was normally 54 beats a minute, but when Dr. Alexander checked it just before the weigh-in, the young Kentuckian's rate had gone up to 120. "Clay is nervous and scared to death and he is burning a lot of energy," said the doctor.

In contrast, Liston's normal resting pulse rate is 72 and it registered 80. The pulse rate and the weight were the only things revealed of the fighters' physical condition by the Commission's physician.

Liston was the first on the scale. He was expected to weigh 215 pounds. "Liston, two hundred and eighteen pounds," Miami Boxing Commissioner Morris Klein shouted to newsmen.

As the champion from Denver stepped off and began putting on his gold-and-white silk robe, Cassius yelled: "Hey, sucker, you're a chump. You've been tricked, chump."

Looking down at Clay and with an ironic but controlled smile, Liston riposted, "Don't let anybody know. Don't tell the world."

"You are too ugly. You are a bear. I'm going to whup you so baaad. You're a chump, a chump . . .", Clay's voice grew shrill. He moved his hands vigorously; he jumped and screamed and his eyes bugged. His body appeared to be shaken. It was startling. It was frightening. But it was an act. There was physical effort involved and probably some fear involved. Yet if Clay was afraid, it was a controlled fear; an energy Clay was accustomed to waste at pre-fight shows.

Commissioner Klein excitedly shouted: "Cassius Clay is fined $2,500 for his behavior on the platform and the money will be withheld from Clay's purse."

Klein said later that he had warned Clay of the fine if he acted up at the weigh-in. "I told him I would tolerate no ranting or raving," the Commissioner concluded.

The afternoon papers in Miami and New York were covered with headlines like: "Hysterical Outburst at Weigh-In," and "Clay Scared," or "Clay Left Fighting at Weigh-In."

"With that kind of fear," protested Dundee, "I'd face a cage of lions. Man, Cassius will win." Dundee said that the scared one was Liston who "was so shook up he couldn't talk. He just didn't know what to make of the kid." However, Jack Nilon, Liston's advisor, had another version of the champion's on-platform remarks. "Sonny said to Clay 'You ain't afraid of me. You're afraid of my left hook,'" said Nilon.

Now it was time for meditation. It was the time when the traditional routine takes effect: rest, quiet, concentration, not too much liquid, the right food (steak, vegetables, a good salad), no distraction and the final touch-up for the fight, which consists of secret messages limited to manager, trainer and fighter. In Clay's case it was Dundee, Bundini, close friend Malcolm X, and personal physician Ferd Pacheco, who checked Clay's pulse rate an hour after the outburst at the weigh-in, finding it back to the normal rate of 54 a minute. Said Pacheco: "He felt Liston would be cautious of a crazy man because Liston didn't know what a crazy man would do. Liston felt that anybody he snarled at should become timid, and this confused him. When he left the weigh-in Clay was almost stoical. He had an almost oriental detachment. He didn't even have to unwind."

Eighty-three hundred people had assembled at the Convention Hall in Miami and 860,000 fans paid up at hundreds of theaters around the world. Clay was a 7–1 underdog. The comedians were having a field day. Joe E. Lewis: "I'm betting on Clay—to live"; Jackie Gleason: "Clay should last about eighteen seconds and that includes the three seconds he brings in the ring with him"; and Joe Louis: "He's got to be kidding!"

But there were a few, just a few, who sensed something. Of the three sportswriters who picked Clay, Leonard Schecter of *The New York Post* wrote, "Anyone who loses to Marty Marshall (the only man to beat Liston) can't be perfect." And one hunch player at local racetrack Hialeah watched a horse named Cassius win the fourth race and pay $19.00, $7.80, and $3.60, and added them all up (1 + 9 + 7 + 8 + 3 + 6) to come up with 34 or 3 + 4 and bet on Cassius in the seventh round.

Before the bell for the first round that evening, February 25, during the pre-fight instructions, Liston stood in the center of the ring, trying to stare the challenger down. Towels tucked under his robe to give his big frame an even more awesome appearance, Liston attempted to intimidate Clay as he had so many others, but Clay stared right back at him and repeated over and over, "Now I've got you, *Chump*."

Then the fight was on. "*He was shuffling that way he does, giving me the evil eye. Man, he meant to kill me, I ain't kidding,*" Clay described it to me years later.

Liston threw the first punch, a long left jab which missed by a foot. Clay was moving backwards and from side-to-side. Liston followed with confidence. Every time Liston threw a punch, Clay was not there. Liston seemed angry. He had only one intention written across his face: murder the kid. Clay, sometimes smiling, would drop his hands and move back, signaling with his hands for Liston to catch up with Clay. "*He missed with a right punch that would have hurt me. I just kept running, watching his eyes. Liston's eyes tip you when he is about to throw a heavy punch. I just watched Liston, so he didn't even sit down. I thought to myself, 'You gonna wish you had rested all you could when we get past this next round.'*"

The second round began like the first, with Clay still dancing around. Liston chasing after Clay. At one point, Liston cornered Clay, but Clay slipped out without trouble and a roar went up from the crowd.

To me, watching, it seemed as if Clay, for the first time since his antic remarks about the fight, had started to believe he could beat Liston. It seemed like a sudden realization. Now he began to snap left jabs at Liston's face.

By the end of the third round, people were humming about the turn this fight was taking. As Liston became gradually discouraged because of his inability to reach Clay, while his face kept receiving stiff jabs, Clay increased his confidence. Clay now stopped and threw a jab, right uppercut, left hook combination. Then just before the bell, with Liston against the ropes, Clay threw a flurry of punches, and Liston had a big gash under the left eye. Clay: *"I knew it was deep, the way the blood spurted right out. I saw his face up close when he wiped his glove at that cut and saw the blood. At that moment, let me tell you, he looked like he's going to look twenty years from now."*

By the fourth round Liston's performance had deteriorated. The pre-fight psychological punches had done damage. Now both believed what Clay had said over and over before the match. "I'm the greatest," Clay whispered to Liston in the fourth round. It was no joke. It wasn't for publicity. Not this time.

But between the fourth and the fifth rounds caustic from Liston's cut got into Clay's eyes. Sitting in his corner, he suddenly couldn't see.

"Cut them off," yelled Clay at Dundee and Bundini, extending his gloves to them. "Please cut them off. I mean it." Then, trying to clear his burning eyes by rubbing his right glove against his face he yelled: "I'm blind." Dundee pushed Clay down. "What are you talking about, man. Are you crazy?" Dundee yelled back at Clay. "This is for the title. Sit down and rest."

"Cut 'em off," Clay cried again. The bell rang and referee Barney Felix was coming to Clay's corner to see what was going on.

At that moment, Dundee was pushing Clay into the middle of the ring.

At that moment a group of blacks who were sitting in the first row began cursing at Dundee. "That white man is trying to blind Clay," one of them yelled. "It's a conspiracy. That white man is with them."

Dr. Ferdie Pacheco, worried about the angry blacks, called up to Dundee for him to wipe the sponge he had used on Clay's eyes in his own to reassure the blacks, and Dundee had to take time from his all-important chores to prove to these strangers that he was not putting on a toxic or blinding substance.

In fact, Dundee's wise and fast action made Clay the world's champion. For Clay got through the fifth round and in the sixth came out throwing punches from every angle and Liston retreated, with blood covering his face. Clay worked Liston over like no other fighter ever had. Liston's eyes became sad. He lost his mean stare. His legs looked weary; his arms seemed to stop. At the bell ending this round, Clay smelled victory. He walked to his corner with his arms and mouth opened.

Everyone but Liston heard the bell for the seventh round. Liston simply stayed down. He was a beaten man. Clay, the first to sense what had happened, began to jump around the ring with his mouth opened. Bundini cried with happiness. Dundee, the man responsible for Clay's victory was all smiles. The fight had followed, almost to the letter, Clay's prediction. He ran around the ring hollering at the reporters: "I told you, I told you—I am the greatest."

Later both fighters spoke to newsmen. Liston first, and then Clay.

The New York Times' Bob Lipsyte wrote: "Arm in sling, bandage under an eye, Liston alternately said that loss of the title made him 'feel like when the President got shot.' And that loss of the title was 'one of those little things that happened to you.' As he left, Terrible Sonny said, 'Thanks, Fellas.'"

"I'm sorry for Liston," Clay told the same newsmen after Liston had left Convention Hall. "You people put too much load on him. You built him up too big and now he has such a long way to fall."

This time newsmen believed Clay. And they listened intently. One reporter remarked, "They sent a boy to do a man's job—and he did it."

CHAPTER 12

February 26, 1964: "Everything with common sense wants to be with his own. Bluebirds with bluebirds, redbirds with redbirds, pigeons with pigeons, eagles with eagles, tigers with tigers, monkeys with monkeys. As small as an ant's brain is, red ants want to be with red ants, black ants with black ants.

"I believe in the religion of Islam, which means I believe there is no God but Allah, and (Elijah) Muhammad is His Apostle. This is the same religion that is believed in by over seven hundred million dark-skinned peoples throughout Africa and Asia.

"I don't have to be what you want me to be. I am free to be who I want."

He didn't take too long to say this. Clay had won the heavyweight crown just the day before. Now he was telling the world he was a member of the Black Muslims.

After Clay's announcement it became known that during promoter Bill MacDonald's efforts to promote the Ali–Liston fight, the promoter had threatened to replace Clay unless "he publicly renounced the Black Muslims and denied his affiliation with them." But encouraged by Malcolm X, who was a constant companion before the Liston fight, Clay told the promoter he was pulling out of the fight. "If that's your condition," he told Mac-Donald, "I won't fight."

The promoter's threat was just what was needed to convince Clay of the Muslims' proclamation that the white man was untrustworthy. And, the promoter, when faced with Clay's threat, withdrew his own. To Clay it was his first indication of "Black Muslim power."

The rest became a matter of public knowledge. The new world's heavyweight champion spoke proudly about how he first became attracted to the Black Muslims.

"Nobody or nothing made me decide. I make up my mind for myself," Clay told me in Miami. "In 1960 in Miami, I was training for a fight. It wasn't long after I had won the 1960 Olympic Gold Medal in Rome. Herb Siler was the fellow I was going to fight. I remember, I put him on the floor in four. Anyway, one day this Muslim minister came to meet me and he asked me, 'Would you like to come to my mosque and hear about the history of our forefathers?' I never had heard no black man talking about no forefathers except that they were slaves so I went to the meeting.

"I was (told that) black people by nature are Muslims and Muslims only means one who submits entirely to the will of Allah—to God. I heard the man preaching (here in Miami, Florida—Second Avenue and Ninth Street—in the black section); as I walked in, he said: 'Elijah Muhammad teaches us that there are no Negroes. Chinese are named after China,' he said; 'Cubans are named after Cuba, Hawaiians are named after Hawaii, Indonesians are named after Indonesia, Puerto Ricans are named after Puerto Rico, Jamaicans are named after Jamaica. Now what country is named "Negroes?" What country is called "Negroes"?' he said. 'Why are we called Negroes?'

"And I said: 'Boy.' That was a shock. That sure makes sense. Why are we called Negroes?

"And he kept saying, 'You don't have your name. Chinese got Chinese names. If I say Mr. Chang-Chung, you know he's a Chinese; if I say he's a Mr. Castro, you know he's a Cuban; if I say here comes Mr. Torres, you know he's a Puerto Rican; if I say here comes Mr. Lumumba, you know he's African.' He said, 'You can identify people from their names. If I say here comes Mr. Pierre, you know he's a Frenchman; if I say here come Mr. Weinstein or Mr. Goldberg, you know he's a Jew; if I say here come Mr. Cole or Mr. Washington or Mr. Smith, you don't know what color he is 'til you see him. You don't know if he's black or white, because all black people in America were named after white people. (And Cassius Clay was a white man in Kentucky, 'cause they got the history on him.)'

"And I said: 'Man, this is something!' That shocked me. He showed me I'm not a Negro and I don't know my name.

"Then he says: 'You don't know your language. Everybody can speak some of their language—Chinese are born in America and never see China, but they can speak some Chinese; Germans are born in America, never see Germany, but they can speak some German; Puerto Ricans are born in America, never seen Puerto Rico, but they can still speak some Spanish. The so-called American Negro, you don't know one word of your true language, you couldn't say "Good morning," to your great grandma if she got out of the grave, because 400 years ago they didn't speak English.' He says, 'If you don't know your name, you don't know your language, you don't know your God, you don't know your religion. The same men who taught you your name, taught you who God was. The same men gave you his language, gave you his religion. You're dead mentally, you know nothing of yourself.

" 'Elijah Muhammad has come from God to teach you a truth (that has) been hidden for 400 years—"Black is beautiful." You are great, your women are great. You can be somebody. Your religion is Islam, your proper God is Allah—he's black, not white.'

" 'Wow,' I said. 'I have to join this thing.'

"But before I joined, I attended a lot of mosque meetings in different places I went. I never did come out of a meeting not understanding something I had not known before. Everywhere I looked, I started seeing things in a new light. Like, I remember right in our house back in Louisville all the pictures on the walls were white people. Nothing about us black people. A picture of a white Jesus Christ. Now, what painter ever saw Jesus? So who says Jesus is white?

"And all my life, I had been seeing the black man getting his head whupped by the white man, and stuck in the white man's jail, and things like that. And myself, I had to admit that up to then, I had always hated being black, just like other Negroes, hating our kind instead of loving one another.

"The more I saw and thought, the more the truth made sense to me. Whatever I'm for, I always believe in talking it up, and the first thing you know, I was in Muslim meetings calling out just like the rest, 'RIGHT, BROTHER! TELL IT BROTHER! KEEP IT COMING!' And today my religion is Islam and I'm proud of it.

"It changed my life in every way. It's pulled me up and cleaned me up as a human being. Before I became a Muslim, I used to drink. Yes, I did. The truth is the truth. And after I had fought and beat somebody, I hadn't hardly go nowhere without two big, pretty women besides me. But my change is one of the things that will mark me as a great man in history. When you can live righteous in the hell of North America, when a man can control his life, his physical needs, his lower self, he elevates himself. The downfall of so many great men is their appetites.

"Now I'm dedicated to Allah, and his prophet (Elijah Muhammad)," Ali said.

He attributes his success to "Allah."

I asked Ali: "What is Allah—is he a human being? Is he black? Is he a spirit? How would you describe him?"

"We were taught that God's spirit is everywhere," Ali said, "but God is a human being, we were taught. That's why we call him 'The Supreme Being.' And this is why we say He made man in His flesh and His image. And He's like a man—this is why we refer to God as 'He, Him and His'—'I want to do His will,' 'He will be seen,' or 'I want to be like Him.' Anything of a male sex, you refer to it as 'He, Him and His.' If God is a spook or spirit they will call it 'the thing' or 'it,' but they refer to God as a man."

"Where is He?"

"Well, if I knew that, I would be God, if I knew where He was. And I don't know.

"But everything on earth was made by man—the jet plane, the moon was put up by men trillions of years ago—wiser than us—and now man's just been out of the cave—the white man's been out of (the) stagecoach 100 years, now he done gone to the moon. If he can go to the moon in 100 years and invent and get that smart, then how much wiser were the people who were here for trillions of years?

"They had time to create and invent bigger things than jets—but all of that was destroyed to let the new man rule. But we believe God's a man. Allah is his name. He taught Elijah Muhammad to teach black people the truth that's been hidden for 400 years."

"Elijah Muhammad spoke to him personally?"

"Yes, God talked to and walked with Elijah Muhammad for three years and a half—that was in Detroit, Michigan—then he left. And the American press did admit a man taught Elijah, a strange visitor from the East (they will admit that), who left America as mysteriously as he came. They do admit that, they won't say he's God, but the white press will admit that a man came and taught Elijah. Elijah said the people didn't know who He was when He was here, but that it was God Himself.

"God said: 'The lost sheep will be found in the last days.' And no people fit the picture of the lost sheep more than Negroes. Everybody's a citizen in America . . . the Negroes can go . . . Africans, Communists—the day after the war in Vietnam, they'll be more free than Negroes, the enemy.

"So, we're the lost sheep that's been found. Today, that's waking up. As the Book says: 'In the last days every man shall return to his own.' This is why you see all the black people wearing Afros, and trying to get back like Africans. You see the white people with hairdos, the long English kind that they used to wear in England. This is the time of separation—not for the worst, but for the best. Every man wants to be with his own kind, marry his own woman. He's a culture. God made us—the birds, the trees, the ants, the animals—everything wants to be with his own. But somebody brainwashed them, don't know who his own is.

"I'm ashamed of myself, but sometimes I've caught myself wishing I had found Islam about five years from now, maybe . . . with all the temptations I have to resist." Ali continues: "But I don't even kiss none, because you get too close, it's almost impossible to stop there. I'm a young man, you know, in the prime of life. Temptations. All types of women, white women too, make passes at me. Girls find out where I live and knock at the door at one and two in the morning. They send me their pictures and phone numbers, saying 'please just telephone me.' They would like to meet me, do I need a secretary? I've even had girls come up here wearing scarves on their heads, with no makeup and all that, trying to act like young Muslim sisters. But the only catch is a Muslim sister never would do that."

It was no longer a secret. Cassius Clay was a Black Muslim. "My name from now on," he told newsmen, "is going to be Cassius X. I will no longer have a slave name."

Angelo Dundee, who never had mentioned his pupil's religion to anyone, revealed his first encounter with the Muslims.

"When Clay was training in the Fifth Street Gym in Miami Beach," Dundee recalls, "for the Liston fight, he had a new pal with him; a big, light-skinned Negro whom he introduced as Sam. That was good enough for me. In boxing we're not too formal. Sam was polite and quiet and friendly. There was another new face in the gym in those days, a face I recognized from the newspaper photos. It was Malcolm X. At the time he was one of the top Muslim leaders.

"One day in the gym, I was standing near Sam when a Negro stranger passed by and called out, 'Hello, Captain Sam.' Captain Sam (Saxon) I soon discovered, was a leader in a Muslim mosque in Miami. I'm told that he helped to convert Clay to the Muslims. Malcolm X was there to complete the conversion."

The reaction was swift. And not positive.

Former heavyweight king Joe Louis said: "Clay will earn the public's hatred because of his connections with the Black Muslims. The things they preach are just the opposite of what we believe. The heavyweight champion should be the champion of all people. He has responsibilities to all people."

Cassius Marcellus Clay, Sr., seeing his grip on his son loosened by the Black Muslims also commented about his son's latest announcement. "He was conned," was the elder Cassius' first reaction. And about his son's demand to be called Cassius X, the old man said: "I'm not changing no name. If he wants to do it, fine. But not me. In fact I'm gonna make good use of the name

Cassius Clay. I'm gonna make money out of my own name. I'll capitalize on it."

Joe Martin, the Louisville patrolman, who first taught the fighter said: "Clay can't get out of the Muslims—he's the one who put them on the front page—they'd kill him."

Bill Faversham described Clay's association with the Muslims with one word: "brainwashed."

"My hopes are that he would come back to us," said Baptist Reverend Mr. Wilson. "Cassius is a good boy. I baptized him when he was nine years old. He and his brother came to visit with me a while back. I talked to them and offered them Christ. I really think Cassius would like to come back but his brother, Rudolph, seemed the stronger of the two. It seemed that his brother was guarding him."

Even writers who had praised Cassius were now putting down Cassius X. One, Jimmy Cannon, even saw Clay's adoption of Muslimism as a "more pernicious hate symbol than (that which) Schmelling and Nazism" had represented in the thirties.

Dr. Martin Luther King, Jr., had some strong words about Clay's revelation. "When Cassius Clay joined the Black Muslims and started calling himself Cassius X," the civil rights leader said, "he became a champion of racial segregation and that is what we are fighting against.

"I think perhaps Cassius should spend more time proving his boxing skill and do less talking."

Former heavyweight king Floyd Patterson went as far as to send Cassius a written challenge. "Cassius, I have admiration for you as a boxer, and feel that you should be a symbol that all Americans should look up to," Patterson wrote. "However, I don't honestly believe what the Black Muslims portray. I am proud to be an American and proud of my people, and no one group of people could make me change my views. Therefore, I challenge you not only for myself, but for all people who think and feel as I do."

Cassius X answered only two fighters who had put down his beliefs in the Black Muslims. About Joe Louis, Cassius said: "Joe Louis was a sucker. Look what happened to him." About Floyd Patterson, Cassius said: "I'll fight Patterson in a winner-take-all bout. I would give my purse to the Black Muslims, and Patterson could give the purse to the Catholic Church if he is the victor.

"I'll play with him for ten rounds. He (Patterson) has been talking about my religion. I will just pow him. Then after I beat him, I'll convert him."

Four weeks after wearing the crown proudly over his head, Cassius X changed his name once more to Muhammad Ali. At the same time, Ed Lassman, President of the World Boxing Association said: "Clay is a detriment to the boxing world. Clay's general conduct," Lassman continued, "is provoking worldwide criticism and is setting a very poor example for the youth of the world. The conduct of the champion before and after winning the title has caused my office to be deluged with letters of torrid criticism from all over the world." Thus spoke the owner of Miami Beach's Wolfie's where Ali ate many times.

Informed of Lassman's statement, Ali fired back: "That's one way you might get me whupped. I didn't hear anything about taking Liston's crown away, last year. Maybe that Lassman guy made a mistake today—maybe he meant Liston, not me.

"I'm an Olympic Gold Medal winner for this country. And I won the heavyweight title fair and clean. Honestly.

"I'm so clean and peaceful, I've never been in any kind of trouble. Lassman's thinking of Liston. I hope they (WBA) won't act like cowards and take it away from me just because they have the power. If they do I'll win it back.

"Furthermore, I don't smoke or drink, and I don't fool around with women. I'm a clean fighter. I've never been in jail and I carry no pistol. I'm an example for the youth of the whole world."

But Cassius Clay had become Muhammad Ali and, worse, he had joined a "violent" and "anti-American militant group" who had organized to "make trouble." The Black Muslims were better known as "the group of blacks who hate whites." The second man in charge, Malcolm X, very instrumental in getting Ali to join the Muslims, was always being described in the newspapers as a former pimp and thief who had spent much of his life in jail and always blamed the white man for whatever was wrong with the world, especially the blacks.

Ali had allied himself with Malcolm, Elijah and the Black Muslims. He had betrayed a segment of whites who were in terror of the Islamic sect. Politicians became outraged.

The fears that whites felt toward the Black Muslims were not altogether paranoid. There was some basis for any white man in America to be concerned, if you were to judge the Muslims by what they preached in their numerous mosques. Yet, I, for one, was not unimpressed by a trip to Harlem.

I was the light heavyweight champion then and Ali invited me and my black manager, Cain Young, to visit his "church." In turn, Ali promised he would come to Young's Baptist church.

I remember being recognized by many of the well-dressed Muslims who were going upstairs to the Mosque in Harlem. Nevertheless, I was frisked and asked to sign a paper which would have me endorse their religion. Young and I didn't sign. It was interesting that when Ali saw me reading the paper he noticed my hesitation and rushed to me. "Don't sign it," he told me. "You have to learn more about what's going on first."

There was a long hall that went from the back of the room straight to the pulpit. To the left of the hall the men sat, to the right, the women, all in long white dresses.

The minister began attacking the Christians. He spoke with anger. "The white man is the devil," he shouted. Many times I found myself nodding my head unconsciously in approval of some of the things that the man in front of me was saying. I was only part black and a Puerto Rican, but it got to me. Two young boys, no more than eight, were in the next row and each time the minister raised his voice to make a point, they would say in unison: "Tell them brother," and "That's right."

But I wasn't too comfortable when the minister said, "Whites have robbed us of everything in the name of their 'law.' They've killed so many times. Their law, the same one that protects them, does not protect us. They have their law—we are looking for our own." I could see where a white man could read that line pretty strong.

By April, two months after winning the crown from Liston and the announcement that there was an understanding for a return bout between the two, the WBA found grounds to strip Ali of his championship. There are no return bout clauses established in the WBA regulations. Obviously, as with the Liston–Patterson rematch, there had been such a private clause when Ali agreed to sign for the first match. (Although the WBA threatened, they took no action in the Liston–Patterson case.) But it was also obvious that people, especially the boxing fan, thought that Liston had lost the first bout by accident, and a second fight would prove fatal for the Black Muslim. New York approved of the match as did California, Massachusetts and Europe.

One day, unexpectedly, while supposedly relaxing in Chicago, the new champion married Sonji Roi, a petite, pretty girl with a golden complexion. And with her, the "greatest," Muhammad Ali went on a trip to Africa.

Hailed as a hero, the first Muslim to win a world championship, he shook hands with such prominent world figures as Egypt's Nasser and Ghana's Nkrumah and was greatly shocked, then titillated with the tremendous welcome he received there.

When he returned from the African tour with his wife Sonji, Ali weighed two hundred and forty-five pounds, the heaviest in his life. And he had a new confidence. For the first time he looked like the Heavyweight Champ.

He began to train for his return bout with Sonny Liston which was set in Boston for November 16, 1964. But three days before the fight, as Dundee was quietly watching a football game on closed-circuit TV, the news came through: Muhammad Ali had been taken to a hospital.

By the time Dundee reached the hospital Ali was in the operating room with an acute hernia. When word reached Liston's camp, Sonny said: "Shit, I worked hard for this fight." Consoling himself, he continued: "But it could have been worse. It could have been me."

Months later, after Ali was out of the hospital and training again, mounting pressure on promoter Sam Silverman by the Veteran committees and the super patriots caused the fight to be canceled in Boston. Silverman was in the red for a reported fifty thousand dollars.

With Ali convalescing from the operation, his syndicate kept looking for feasible alternatives. An offer came from Lewiston, an unknown town in Maine. The syndicate grabbed the offer and the Ali–Liston match became alive again.

The training began again and fifteen months after winning the championship, Ali stepped up to face "The Big, Ugly Bear," for the second time. I was a new champion, two months old myself and went to cover the Ali–Liston bout for a Spanish radio station in New York. I was broadcasting the fight for a delayed program.

The night before, I was with Liston in his hotel room, illustrating to him how I had beaten Willie Pastrano by cutting the ring short. He promised me he would do the same to Ali.

On the night of May 25, 1965, at about 10:30 P.M., Sonny Liston and Muhammad Ali had a contest of stares while referee and former world's heavyweight champion Jersey Joe Walcott gave the instructions in the middle of the ring.

Two minutes later, the fight was over, with Ali walking around the ring with his arms spread to the ceiling and Sonny Liston still groggy and shocked in one corner of the ring.

But it was a night of confusion for the fans and of disappointment to me.

Liston came out and began to press Ali, but with seemingly reluctant steps. When Ali stopped, he stopped too. He just followed Ali around trying to hit him with jabs. Ali moved around smiling while Liston's eyes appeared to have rays of fire in them. Suddenly, Liston remembered his promise to me. And just at that moment when he took the first step to cut the ring short, Liston made the mistake of throwing a slow jab. Ali took a step back, moving his head three inches to his right and just as Liston's jab scraped the left side of Ali's face, Ali let go a swift straight right. Liston's eyes never saw the punch.

His body fell as quickly as the punch had landed. As Walcott tried to start the count, Ali remained excitedly near the fallen body, not complying with the boxing regulation of going to a neutral corner. By the time referee Walcott persuaded Ali to walk to a neutral corner, Nat Fleischer, Publisher of *Ring Magazine*, claimed that Liston had been on the floor over the necessary ten seconds. Fleischer called Walcott to the side and immediately signaled the former champion to stop the fight. Walcott returned to the center of the ring where Liston and Ali were now swinging at each other.

Walcott simply walked toward Ali and raised his arm while Liston watched in astonishment. Fans began screaming: "Fix, fix."

The producer of my show, Nahro Diaz, began to scream with the crowd. "That's right," he said, "it was a fix."

I was so emotionally involved with the mood of he crowd that I had forgotten what I had seen. But I had the tape recorder with me. I played it back and heard myself saying: ". . . a perfect shot to the jaw, right on the button and Liston is down. He's badly hurt. He might not get up."

You see, that was a perfect example of a punch that causes a separation of the senses. The punch was not what one could call powerful. Instead, it was its quickness, its sharpness, and its accuracy which caused the knockout. These ingredients made the punch invisible to Liston. Unable to see the punch, Liston's mind could not function to prepare him for the impact.

I spoke to both fighters minutes after the fight. Liston admitted to me that he saw the punch "too late."

Ali told me that he hit Liston's oncoming face with a perfect shot to the chin. "I felt it right here," he said pointing to his right shoulder.

The following day most of the newspapers I read, spoke about how Liston had fallen from a "phantom punch," and then went on to state that he was much older than he claimed to be. They had forgotten the columns they had written not so long ago about his invincibility.

But Sonny Liston had lost both of his fights with Ali for the same reason: he was psyched out in both fights. Liston, in my estimation, quit in both fights. In the first, because initially he was completely frustrated, and then became discouraged; in the second, it was his subconscious mind. Deep down, in the innermost part of his soul, Sonny Liston feared Muhammad Ali. And, even more, he feared the Black Muslims.

Another man who seemed terrified of the Black Muslims was Floyd Patterson, who made a statement which indicated his dislike for them. In a letter published in various newspapers, Floyd deplored the fact that boxing had a heavyweight champion who did not consider himself a representative of America. "I am willing to fight for nothing if necessary," Floyd said, "just so I can bring the championship back to America." That statement was well received by white America and Patterson became the first black "white hope" in boxing history.

Floyd, a recent convert to Roman Catholicism, was trying to get his fifth chance to regain the crown he won on November 30, 1956, when he became the youngest heavyweight king in boxing's history. Three years later, Patterson lost his crown to Ingemar Johansson. Then nine months after being dethroned, Floyd made history again by knocking out Johansson, becoming the first heavyweight champion to regain his title.

Floyd finally lost his crown again for good when Liston disposed of him twice, consecutively, both times in round one.

But now, after insulting Ali's religious beliefs and the Black Muslims, Floyd got another chance to make history. And it was not that easy for him to do, since Floyd, after being humiliated by Liston not once, but twice, went into hiding for months.

He admitted later that he came to see my championship fight in a disguise, two months before his scheduled fight with Ali.

But a few weeks before making the match, Ali, as usual, counterattacked Floyd's remarks. "The only reason Patterson's decided to come out of his shell," Ali said in *Playboy* magazine, "is to try and make himself a big hero to the white man by saving the heavyweight title from being held by a Muslim.

"I wish you would print for Patterson to read that if he ever convinces my managers to let him in the same ring with me, it's going to be the first time I ever trained to develop in myself a brutal killer instinct. I've never felt that way about nobody else. Fighting is just a sport for me, a game to me. But Patterson I would want to beat to the floor for the way he rushed out of hiding after his last whupping, announcing that he wanted to fight me because no Muslim deserves to be the champ.

"I never had no concern about his having the Catholic religion. But he was going to jump up to fight me because he wants to be the white man's champion. And I don't know of a sadder example of nobody making a bigger fool of himself."

Muhammad Ali went on to explain about the recent problem Floyd had with his home in a white neighborhood in New York, where Floyd lived with his family. The house was for sale after a confrontation with a neighbor whose children called Floyd's children "niggers."

"I ain't never read nothing more pitiful than how Patterson told the newspapers, 'I tried to integrate . . . it just didn't work,' " Ali said. "It is like when he was the champion," Ali continued, "the only time he would be caught in Harlem was when he was in the back of a car waving in some parade. The big shot didn't have no time for his own kind, he was so busy integrating. And now he wants to fight me because I stick up for black people. I'll tell him again, he sure better think five or six times before he gets in a ring with me."

A couple of weeks after the *Playboy* interview both Patterson and Ali signed a contract to fight on November 22, 1965, in Las Vegas. Ali called Floyd "the rabbit." His antics began. One day as Floyd was training at his home, Ali came for a visit.

I was there and I remember when Ali, with a pack of carrots for the "rabbit" walked into Floyd's training quarters and began taunting him. At one point a reporter asked Floyd: "Do you get mad with these things?"

"Well, I'm happy that the heavyweight champ, Mister Clay, took time to . . ."

"That ain't my name," Ali shouted. "You know my name. C'mon rabbit, what's my name?"

"I was saying," Floyd started again, "that I was happy to see Ali . . ."

"The full name," demanded Ali. "I didn't hear you calling me by my full name."

"Well, Cassius Clay is the name he was born with," Floyd said.

"Don't be mad at me," Ali shouted. "I'm not the white man who chased you out from that white neighborhood."

The dialogue went on and on more or less in this fashion. The following day the New York press played it up in the sports pages as if Jack Johnson had been resuscitated.

I watched the fight on closed-circuit and saw how Ali literally destroyed Floyd. In the first round, Ali didn't throw one punch. He just moved, bent, pulled back and invited Floyd to throw punches while Ali had his hands down. It was sheer humiliation. Floyd's tense inability to land any blows must have put knots in his back.

In the third round, Floyd's sacroiliac went on him. I knew he had had a bad back long before this fight when we were both managed by Cus D'Amato. I had seen many times how Cus would work on his back to get it in place. This time, Cus was at ringside almost tempted to go up in the ring and help, even though Patterson had eased Cus out. Not a bitter man with his fighters, Cus painfully watched how one of Floyd's cornermen worsened Floyd's back condition.

The fight had one pattern. It was Ali throwing punches, many of them hitting Floyd. Every time Floyd tried to punch, his face would twist with pain. People at ringside were yelling at the referee to stop the torture. Most people thought that Ali was purposely trying not to knock Floyd out in order to make him suffer. A sadistic performance.

But I didn't feel this way. I thought Ali couldn't knock Floyd out. With his back out of place, and no chance to win the fight, Floyd concentrated on defense, making sure to take a good look at every punch Ali threw. He did just that until the twelfth round when referee Harry Krause stopped the one-sided match.

A few days later Floyd told me: "José, Clay hit me right on the chin, not once but many times. I didn't feel the damn punches. He can't punch." For a man who had a reputation of having a glass chin, Floyd's remarks were quite significant, I thought, especially for my theory of the knockout.

In his book, *Soul on Ice*, Eldridge Cleaver saw the fight this way: "The simplistic version of the fight bandied about in the press was that there was a 'white hope' and a 'black hope' riding on this fight. The white hope for a Patterson victory was, in essence, a counterrevolutionary desire to force the Negro, now in rebellion and personified in the boxing world by Ali, back into his 'place.' The black hope, on the contrary, was to see Lazarus crushed, to see Uncle Tom defeated, to be given symbolic proof of the victory of the autonomous Negro over the subordinate Negro."

Cleaver went on to say that other puppets would emerge to try to defeat Ali, but the author admitting, in effect, that Ali was not a perfect human being, said of him, ". . . a free man determined not to be a white man's puppet, even though he fights to entertain them."

CHAPTER 13

L et us go back a little. On a hot January day in 1964, just days after his 22nd birthday, and one month before his first match with Sonny Liston, Number 15-47-42-127 sat in a room at an Army Induction Center in Coral Gables, Florida, studying the questions:

"A shopkeeper divided a number by 3.5 when the number should have been multiplied by 4.5. His answer is 3. What should the correct answer be?"

"(a) 5.25 (b) 10.50 (c) 15.75 (d) 47.25"

"A vendor was selling apples for $10 a basket. How much would you pay for a dozen baskets if one-third of the apples have been removed from each of the baskets?"

(a) $10 (b) $30 (c) $40 (d) $80"

"When I looked at a lot of the questions they had on them Army tests, I just didn't know the answers," Clay said. "I didn't even know how to start after finding the answers."

He missed enough of these questions to score 16 percentile in the Armed Forces Qualifying Test. Since a passing mark was 30 percentile, he was classified 1-Y.

Then the Army gave him another test two months later in Louisville. Same results. ("I said I was the greatest, not the smartest.")

Clay had registered for the draft on April 18, 1960, two months after his 18th birthday, with Local Board No. 47 in Louisville, Kentucky, immediately before embarking for Rome and the Olympics. "I was a Christian at the time . . . I knew nothing about Islam. I was Cassius Clay. I wasn't Muhammad Ali. I had no knowledge of Elijah Muhammad or Islam and if you had drafted me that day I would have went."

He was classified 1-A on March 9, 1962, and almost a year later, just a few weeks before the first Liston fight, was ordered to report for his physical in Miami. "I didn't tell them that I was a conscientious objector, but I did write my name 'Cassius X' on the paper. When the official asked me why I did that I explained the religion (I had wrote 'Islam' instead of 'Christianity') and the Nationality (put down 'Asiatic Blackman' instead of 'Negro') and he asked me to come into the back room. He then gave me a list of about 300 organizations and said 'Do you belong to any of these? They are subversive groups,' or something like that. And I said, 'I don't belong to none of them. I'm a Muslim,' but he didn't have Islam on the list." Since this interview coincided with his mark of 16, he was comfortably deferred for the time.

But two years later, on February 17, 1966, three months after he had humiliated Floyd, Ali was relaxing on the lawn of his rented home in Miami, when a reporter came to tell him that the pass-percentile had been dropped to 15, making him eligible and so he had been reclassified 1-A by his local Louisville draft board and would be called up for service shortly.

As television mobile units maneuvered to capture his reactions, Ali reacted.

"How can they do this without another test to see if I'm wiser or worser than last time? Why are they gunning for me? I ain't got no quarrels with them Viet Congs."

That last statement couldn't have been made at a worse time.

February 17th was the same day that General Maxwell Taylor had answered Senator Wayne Morse's attack on the war in Southeast Asia by stating that Hanoi would be only too pleased with such dissension in the U.S.

Ali was catapulted into the headlines in hours, and called a "Tool of Hanoi."

During the years Ali was classified as 1-Y and busy defending his newly-won championship, his local Louisville draft board received over 1,000 letters from all over the country condemning the draft board. Some of the samples: "You are still cowards, eh? Send that nigger away."; "That nigger is no better than anybody else. Draft his ass."; "How much has Clay paid you to keep him out of the Army? You had better resign before some soldier takes a shot at you. You are nothing but a 'yellow belly Negro lover' and apparently a 'cheap Jew' "; "How come his African ancestors ride around in Cadillacs? Let's not discriminate or has King been threatening and using his blackmail tactics?"; and "When are you going to have the guts to bring that lousy loud-mouthed, un-American, cowardly, nigger back home and put him in the Army where we all hope he'll have his head shot off?"

The late Congressman Mendel Rivers of South Carolina was threatening an investigation of the entire Selective Service System in general and Louisville in particular, and the citizenry wasn't particularly behind Ali in his stand against the draft.

There is a legacy in boxing. It's the legacy of "tank jobs," where a fighter takes a dive. And it's the legacy of the old-fashioned criminal "syndicate." What was left of the Mob in boxing felt threatened by someone moving in on their territory: the Black Muslims.

For even if Ali's contract had nine more months to run with the Louisville sponsoring group, he still was putting together a promotional group that for the first time included blacks. And that threatened the structure. After all, wasn't this a sport where blacks worked in the ring and whites collected for their physical hurts?

With the heavyweight championship of the world such a valuable piece of property, it was only natural that the old fight mob would have its champion—WBA Champion Ernie Terrell—to hold a piece of their place in the boxing hierarchy against the Black Muslims who had Muhammad Ali to challenge the power system. There were not only two champions, but two social structures colliding. To complicate the situation further, just as Ali had provoked the country with his last remark, so was Terrell in trouble then. The proposed Ali–Terrell fight for the undisputed heavyweight championship of the world had already been installed in Chicago after having been moved out of New York. For Terrell, a very tall boxer whose talents could be summed up in two words—left jab—had been seen in undesirable company, and the company called "detrimental to boxing" had accompanied Terrell to New York from Chicago. The "undesirable" was Bernie Glickman, friend not only to Ernie, but to Frankie Carbo, Blinkie Palermo and a few other Chicago and New York members of that underworld which always settles in around boxing.

Glickman's appearance on the same plane with Terrell en route to the hearing didn't go down well with the New York Commission. They had denied the Chicago-based fighter a license, also irritating a few mobsters who felt Glickman had "queered" the fight. Subsequently, they made threats on Glickman's life and beat him up.

After this respectable inauguration of the fight, it was quickly moved to Chicago, but now in the wake of Ali's "Viet Cong" remark, the possibility of the fight being held anywhere in Chicago (or America) was jeopardized.

Under the Illinois Sports Act, which forbids "moral turpitude or action detrimental to boxing on the part of (any) fighters," the Illinois Athletic Commission now investigated whether Ali's remark might not be so defined.

Governor Otto Kerner convened a new conference to label Ali's remarks "disgusting." Even more harmful was the reaction to Ali's statement from the man on the fifth floor of City Hall, Mayor Daley. "I hope it won't be held in Chicago, and I am confident the Commission will take the proper action." The fight was banned, pending a hearing.

Back in Florida, Ali was, at first, content to add to the fire: "If they'd just let me fight, I would pay for two modern fighter planes in two fights, or I could pay the salaries of 100,000 men."

Then, at the urging of his new manager, Herbert Muhammad, the Son of "God" and a Chicago resident who understood the powers of the white "God," Mayor Daley, Ali made a phone call to the Commission Chairman asking for permission to come to Chicago.

According to the Chairman, Ali asked permission to apologize to the Governor, the Commission, and to the public "for having his big mouth make the statements he did."

One of the three commissioners, Lou Radzienda, said: "This is all becoming a kindergarten situation. In my opinion, if the Commission rejects the fight, the attorneys for Terrell and Clay would have a legal recourse. This country is fighting for freedom all over the world. And part of this freedom is for a man to say what he wants."

But freedom of speech was not what the public wanted, especially when they had to give it to a black man who refused to fit into the role traditionally prescribed for a black heavyweight champion.

When Ali showed up at the hearing to—in words of the Commissioner—"apologize," he defended his statements. He only apologized for saying them to the press instead of to the Commission.

"I'm not here for a showdown and I'm not here in the way the press said I would. I received a phone call in Miami from certain advisers, who I trust, who told me that people would be hurt financially by my beliefs and convictions and that you (the Commissioners) and other people had been put on the spot by the governor and other high authorities. I am here to offer my apologies for what embarrassment and pressures I have put you under.

"I apologize for saying to newspaper reporters what should have been taken up with officials from the draft board. I apologize for opening my mouth and saying these things to the wrong people."

But Clay was not responsive to the question, "Did he apologize for the 'unpatriotic remarks' he had made, regardless of who he said them to?"

"I'm not apologizing for nothing like that, because I don't have to."

Then, claiming that the Commissioners were taunting him by continually calling him "Mr. Clay," Muhammad Ali walked out of the hearing and, effectively, out of Illinois.

The vote came out 2–1, a foregone conclusion, banning the fight in Illinois. One of the two members voting against the fight was a black man. (The Commission defended itself by letting it be known that they felt there was something "kinky" about the fight.)

The promoters, Main Bout, now took the fight back home to Louisville, where the city fathers also banned the fight, then on to Pittsburgh, then to Bangor, Maine, and finally, Huron, South Dakota. But even in such "water stops," the fight was unwelcome. Finally, the promoters took the fight north of the border to Canada. But it was no easier to find a place there.

The bout was first announced for Montreal, then called off, as "The New Orleans of the North" took umbrage at being the site of a "second-hand" fight. Then it went to its suburb, Verdun. Then to faraway Edmonton, then to a little river port town called Sorel in Quebec. Finally, it came to rest in Toronto.

Then Ernie Terrell pulled out. He claimed a "contract dispute." Terrell's advisers had counseled him to pull out. Only three things could happen now, they figured—One: Ali would win and they'd lose everything; Two: Ali would be drafted and either go into the service, or refuse induction and go to jail—in either case leaving Terrell as the only "champion" left; or Three: Terrell would fight and win, but for a comparatively small purse. Why, therefore, risk Terrell's WBA title, especially when recourse had already been sought in the courts to prevent Ali from calling himself the "heavyweight champion"?

So Ernie picked up his guitar and went home.

But now, with a March 29th date and a site and an arena, Main Bout was not about to forego putting Ali in the ring against someone. So they decided George Chuvalo was ready to fight for the title. At least he was a local Toronto boy.

Called "the Washerwoman" by Ali ("Did you ever see him swing? He throws his arms around just like a washerwoman."), Chuvalo had been promised a shot at the title once before.

When Chuvalo fought Floyd Patterson in February of 1965, the newly-crowned Champ said, "If you can defeat 'The Rabbit' and look good in defeating him, I may give you an opportunity to be in a $10 million gate with me."

Ali, hired as a commentator for the Chuvalo–Patterson fight for $10,000 stole the show with his quotes, his antics, and finally the wreck of his new $10,500 bus, "Big Red," with thirty newsmen aboard, en route to Chuvalo's training camp in the Catskills, where fighters have trained for thirty years, since the days of Barney Ross. ("All whites to the rear, this is a segregated bus.") Another time, he walked into Chuvalo's camp with a mop and pail and presented them to the Toronto heavyweight.

Now the Toronto heavyweight was going to fight before his hometown fans for the Heavyweight Championship of the world.

Or was that impossible?

Ontario was member of the World Boxing Association which officially recognized Ernie Terrell as their heavyweight champion and Zora Folley as the Number One contender. Therefore, while the fight was for the championship of the world, it was *not* for the championship of Ontario, and was advertised as "a heavyweight showdown," with Ali as "the people's champ" and Chuvalo as "Canada's Champ."

The fight nobody wanted was financially doomed from the start. Ali's remark had generated a brushfire of patriotism unseen in America since Pearl Harbor, and this, coupled with his unpopular religion, had shrunk a potential $3 million closed-circuit promotion into one that would be lucky to gross a half-million.

In fact, closed-circuit locations were being closed by the local VFW's and American Legion groups, making the total number of viewers in closed-circuit theaters the smallest of the electronic age. And, only 7,500 paid an estimated $125,000, far below even the pessimistic expectations.

Chuvalo, however, who had never been floored or stopped in his 48-bout career, made a fight of it.

Ali never even came close to flooring the granite-chinned contender whose best attack was, in the words of one reporter, "a left chin to the right glove."

Chuvalo took everything that Ali could throw round-after-round, and in fact, only once, in the eleventh round, when he went all out to bring his strong opponent to his knees, did Ali even succeed in making the Canadian back up. Chuvalo's most consistent offense was below Ali's belt. His many foul punches went without any warnings or penalties from referee Jack Silvers, who explained his action (or inaction) by saying: "They were not deliberate. Chuvalo is a body puncher—that's his style." Thus, Silvers, as much as Chuvalo "made" the fight, betrayed a lack of neutrality unseen in many a year.

But for Ali it was a one-sided victory over a human punching bag, with a high threshold of pain. He lost only two rounds on even the closest official's card (referee Silver's) and lost just one round on the other two cards.

Drew "Bundini" Brown, who had been fired by Ali after the second Liston fight, trained Chuvalo for the fight, and sat at ringside yelling, "Think of yo' babies," to Chuvalo, father of four.

Joe Louis was also in Chuvalo's corner, adding both a promotional lift to the hexed fight and fuel to the fire of black nationalists, who now saw their old hero in a white man's corner.

Ali, who was induced to fighting for the smallest payoff to a defending champion since Jersey Joe Walcott received only $92,000 to defend against Ezzard Charles back in 1952, suffered one more indignity after the fight: the Canadian Government withheld his purse to insure his payment of taxes.

Now, with a draft call-up facing him almost immediately, Ali began searching for another quick fight.

Main Bout worked out a tour through Europe for the fighter who was too hot to handle in America.

In London, on May 26, 1966, Ali faced the man who had put him on the canvas three years before. Veteran Henry Cooper had his second chance to repeat the feat of knocking Ali down, but with the double difference that this time Ali was world's champion and Cooper had the idea he would hit the champ harder so he could remain on the canvas over ten seconds.

But as in their first encounter, blood flowed out of Cooper's cuts and the English fighter couldn't continue after the sixth round. He never came close to hurting Ali, who as world's champion had developed a confidence and will he didn't have three years ago. Now the English press said that Clay could be compared with the best of the heavyweights in boxing history.

Three months later, on August 6, in the same ring where he had disposed of Cooper, Ali faced Brian London, a man who had been demolished by Patterson and who the American boxing people referred to as the "live punching bag."

After receiving a beating for three rounds and living up to his American nickname, London fell unconscious at the end of the third round.

A month later, on September 10, Ali traveled to Germany and squared off against a seemingly easy opponent, Karl Mildenberger. But when Ali walked to the middle of the ring, Mildenberger waited for him with a *right* jab. It was the first time in his pro career that Ali had to look at such a punch. Karl was a southpaw, and not a bad fighter. From the beginning, Ali seemed to have trouble in solving his opponent's stance. After a change of patterns all through the fight, Ali finally found a formula and started to move to his own left instead of toward his right. He also began moving less and pressing once in a while.

By round twelve, Ali knocked the German out, in one of the tougher fights of his career.

But one thing Ali had done in Europe: he had eliminated every heavyweight Europe could offer. So there was no other place to go but back to America.

A few months after his return Ali decided to step in against Cleveland Williams, a big, powerful man who had given Sonny Liston a tremendous fight a few years back.

Recently shot by a Houston cop and surviving an emergency operation, Williams came into the Astrodome ring on the night of November 16, 1966, to demolish Muhammad Ali. I also saw this fight a few days after on film.

Of course, watching a fight in a movie is not the same as being there. One can't feel the power of the punches, and the reaction of the fighters becomes deceptive. But one can observe the ability to punch and the keenness of good defense.

I remember Williams coming to the center of the ring with Ali dancing around him. In the first, Ali moved with his hands low. At times he stopped, hands up, and would jab; stiff jabs.

Round two found Muhammad Ali at his best. It was a show of art, a spectacle for every boxing man to see. That night at about ten-thirty, no one in the history of this loved and hated sport could have beaten Muhammad Ali, much less Cleveland Williams.

In the third round, Ali came out taunting Williams. Standing right in front of him, Ali fired rapid, stiff jabs. He would step back, then dart back in again with murderous left and right combinations. At one point, Ali threw a combination of five flashy punches, each making contact with Williams's groggy face. Williams dropped. The fight was over. It was Ali's best performance.

After that fight, I was convinced no heavyweight could have beaten him. What many people in the game called luck, was, in fact, the work of a genius who could convert fear into energy.

Thinking that Mildenberger had given Ali a tough fight because of his awkward style, the structure controlling the "other champion," Ernie Terrell, now decided that Terrell had the most unorthodox style in America, and that he possessed a jab similar if not better than Ali's. The match that didn't get put on before, now materialized fast enough.

Three months after his magnificent exhibition against Cleveland Williams, on February 6, 1967, the two champions met surrounded by an all-time attendance record of 37,321 paying customers at the Astrodome in Houston.

"I will not freeze like Williams," said the Octopus, as Ali named Terrell, "or panic like Sonny Liston. He's been trying to psych me and psyching is an indication of lack of confidence. If Cassius is going to beat me up as bad as he says he is, he should keep quiet or I might not show up."

At the sound of the first gong, Terrell came out and threw a jab that missed. The people watching the fight at the Academy of Music Theater in Manhattan began to laugh even as Ali began laughing at Terrell, who kept missing jabs and sloppy right shots.

By the fifth round, everyone knew who the winner was going to be. Ali's superiority was obvious. It was not a good fight to watch.

At the end of fifteen rounds we heard Terrell saying how good a fighter Ali was. The only good Ali could have gotten from that fight was his ability to cope with any style. If he lost two rounds against Terrell they were two too many. I think the only thing worrying Ali that night was that the Army had set a date for him to report for induction.

Working fast, against the clock, Ali signed to fight 34-year-old World Boxing Association number one contender, Zora Folley, who had accused Floyd Patterson of evading him when Floyd was the champ. The match was set for Madison Square Garden for March 22, 1967, a month after the Terrell episode.

The Ali–Folley match marked the fight as the first heavyweight championship match in New York since Patterson had knocked out Ingemar Johansson back in 1960. For the Garden, it was its first heavyweight title match since 1951.

Clay was to get fifty percent of everything; Folley fifteen percent of the loot.

"Folley's such a nice man with eight children," said Ali, "I'm glad he's gettin' a payday."

Folley, a veteran top contender for the last ten years, with a record of seventy-one victories, seven defeats and four draws, walked into the ring pale, with deep, sad eyes. He was the first experienced fighter I ever saw looking terrified.

The first round began with Folley chasing Ali carefully. Ali, as usual, confident of a victory, dropped his hands and began to move his legs with such delicacy and class that it was an enjoyment to watch him. Then he became mean. He started in the second round to jab Folley with stiff jabs. Only his left.

In the third round, Folley with the same lack of confidence he had had walking into the ring, began trying to sneak punches. It was embarrassing. Ali would make him miss and then reply with three or four jabs. In the fourth, a punch dropped Folley.

In the fifth round, Ali began to apply pressure by continuing to use his stiff jabs and a continued feint. By round six people began to walk out of the Garden. Folley seemed to be looking for the place to fall as Ali began his final attack. When the bell sounded ending round six, Folley walked to his corner with a sorrowful, defeated look on his face. And in the next round, Ali unleashed a savage attack, then stepped back coolly.

Folley, who was looking for an incentive to fight or to fall, seemed to have a question in his eyes. "Let me hit you, please, or knock me out." The champ got the message. Ali walked toward Folley who made the motion of throwing a left jab. As his body moved toward Ali, the champ's right hand was coming. Jaw and fist met. And the jaw was the loser, taking Zora Folley with it to the floor.

Muhammad Ali was still the heavyweight king. But three weeks after retiring Zora Folley, on April 28, 1967, there came an hour when he was obliged to keep his word. He refused to take the traditional step at his United States Army induction. Now Ali's opponent became the strongest of them all: the United States Establishment.

CHAPTER 14

On April 28, 1967, as he had announced in advance, Ali refused induction into the Armed Forces. The reaction of the politicians was quick. The World Boxing Association and the New York State Athletic Commission didn't wait. Almost instantly they stripped Ali of the crown he had won in the ring long before his conviction in the lower courts.

Three months after the WBA took Ali's title, they created an elimination to pick its next champion, but almost every member of the "elimination tournament" had been knocked out by Ali. Sonny Liston was not included, while Frazier refused to participate.

"Let them have the elimination bouts," Ali told the *Houston Post*. "Let the man that wins go to the backwoods of Georgia and Alabama or to Sweden or Africa. Let him stick his head in an elementary school, let him walk down a back alley at night. Let him stop under a street lamp where some small boys are playing and let him say: 'What's my name?' and see what they say. Everybody knows me and knows I am the champion.

"You see, they know who the real champion is and all the rest is sparring partners."

With lawyers in New York trying to get his boxing license back but with every such effort exhausted, Muhammad Ali began losing hope for his return. By the end of 1967 he was saying that he was going to buy a few farms and become a farmer.

But by now part of America was enraged with what the "system" had done to Ali. The Vietnam war had become more and more unpopular, America's youth was restless and the Black Muslims were growing in influence among the blacks and appearing more respectable to the whites. So Muhammad Ali's popularity also began go grow. The second most important Black Muslim in America, he began preaching in Muslim mosques.

When his need for money began giving him trouble, Ali commenced speaking at colleges and rallies. At one point he became a stage actor in a play called *Buck White*, which had seven performances on Broadway before closing down.

But Muhammad Ali, who had made millions in the boxing rings, couldn't keep up with his expenses, especially the twelve hundred dollars a month alimony he had to pay to his first wife, Sonji.

On August 17, 1967, Ali married again, but this time to a Black Muslim girl who wouldn't offer Ali the same show of independence which had forced his first marriage to a divorce, ten months after the wedding.

Sonji, and Ali's second wife, Belinda Boyd, were different souls. Sonji couldn't adjust to Ali's Black Muslim belief, while Belinda, 17, was born in the religion, worked in a bakery store near the Chicago Mosque and had never been in a movie house, never used "stuff" on her face. She had been a full-time, genuine Black Muslim all of her life.

With boxing hurt by Ali's absence, promoters around the country missed Ali. Some of them began doing some underground work to bring him back. Some of the liberal politicians began to offer comments about Ali, and they were in his favor. Bobby Kennedy once said to me that he thought it was a crime what "we" were doing to the man who had been deprived of practicing his trade.

The long struggle began. Mike Malitz and Harold Conrad, Main Bout's two principals, began having conversations with political figures in different states. "Every time," Conrad recalls, "we had finished with the preliminaries, word would leak out and we were dead."

Because of the money he had spent in this legal battle against conviction for his refusal to serve in the Armed Forces, there was an announcement on September 28, 1968, that Ali would fight some exhibition matches in Columbus, Ohio. His first wife immediately began putting on pressure. A plumber who had done a job at his Philadelphia house was reported to have come to Ali's door with a check that bounced. "I'm sorry," Ali was reported as saying, "but that's the way it is. Have no money."

Yet, Ali's integrity was impenetrable. When in all this financial trouble, a movie company offered Ali four hundred thousand dollars to play Jack Johnson in a film, he refused. "I wouldn't appear on no screen with no white woman," he said, and refused to discuss the matter.

Even from Havana came word that Castro wanted Ali to be interviewed by the communist radio station. So, after everything was set, Ali got on the phone and the interview began. "They wanted to know about Vietnam, the American government and the white people," Ali told me years later. "I said to them, 'You pay me for this and I might be able to answer all those questions. No money, no answer.' The man at the other end said, 'Okay, Mister Money. We now know a little more about you.'"

At one point during his exile, it was announced by a national poll that Muhammad Ali was the most sought-after speaker in the United States, after Senators Edmund Muskie and Edward Kennedy. Around this time, Ali began getting paid by the Black Muslims themselves on his speaking engagements around the different mosques.

Refusing to do what Jack Johnson once did: to jump bail and flee to another country, Ali remained here. When his lawyers tried to get permission for him to fight abroad, permission was denied. Furthermore, his passport was revoked. He was under bail.

Bundini remembers when there was talk that Ali might fight Frazier in Miami. "We went to Florida on three different occasions, but we was disappointed." Speaking of the poor sums offered, Bundini said, "He was supposed to fight for marijuana there. First some promoters said they had Frazier signed up. Then they said they had Ellis. And him (Ali) and his wife and me didn't have no money at all. We was eatin' out of the same pot. Then we was supposed to go to Charleston, South Carolina, and a couple of other places. And sometimes the champ couldn't afford to pay me. And I was with him then. I even went with him on his college tours."

Angelo Dundee remembers when Ali, during this exile, almost fought Patterson in Las Vegas. "Everything was set," said Angelo, "and I always kidded Ali that I had to make a lot of money quick so I could put a swimming pool for my kids behind the new home I had in Miami. When the news comes that the fight is off, Ali is sitting on the bed, and he's quiet for a while and then he says: 'Angelo, it don't look like you're gonna get that swimming pool.' Imagine him thinking of that then."

Ali remained tough with his decision that he was right when he refused to take the traditional step. "The power structure seems to want to starve me out," he said on a television program. "I mean the punishment, five years in jail, ten-thousand-dollars fine, ain't enough. They want to stop me from working, not only in the country but out of it. Not even a license to fight an exhibition for charity. And that's in the Twentieth Century. You read about these things in the dictatorship countries where a man don't go along with this thing or that and he's completely not allowed to work or to earn a decent living. So this is my position. But I rely on Allah. I leave it up to Allah."

From 1968 to 1970 promoters tried to get Ali to fight in Tampa and Orlando; in Macon, Georgia; in Seattle, Pittsburgh, and Detroit, in Hot Springs, Arkansas; Columbus, Ohio; and Austin, Texas; in Jackson, Mississippi. Even in Sacaton, Arizona, the Gila River Indians refused to allow Ali to fight on their reservation due to "their military and historical heritage."

The only way Ali got into a ring was by a computerized tournament in which out of a comparison of records, Ali was defeated by James J. Jeffries. Ali sued the Florida corporation for making the computerized results public because, as his lawyer put it, "Ali suffered a low blow to his reputation and prestige, and should be compensated for same to the tune of one million dollars." Never defeated by a professional fighter, Ali said, "They won't let me fight to earn a living anymore, and my name is all I've got. Now somebody is trying to ruin that, too."

Every time Ali accused someone of interfering with him he said, "they" meaning the Establishment, or white people. But some of "they" actually began to work to get Ali back in the ring.

A white man named Harry Pett, head of a spice-processing firm in Atlanta, was told by his son-in-law, Bob Kassel, also white, who had recently been involved with Malitz and Conrad in the Frazier–Ellis title bout, that he was sure to get the Ali–Frazier fight for Atlanta if he could get Ali a permit. The fight, Kassel told Pett, could draw over five million dollars.

Pett, who Ali would have described as a man "with the right complexion," called his black friend, Leroy Johnson. Now, Johnson didn't have the "right complexion," but he certainly had the *right connection*, for he was the same politician who in 1962 had become the first black man to be elected to office in Atlanta in ninety-two years. Senator Leroy Johnson began to pull his strings.

The Senator is a shrewd politician who had helped Sam Massell become the first Jewish mayor of Atlanta by getting ninety percent of the black vote for him. Johnson knew politics in his town. If he endorsed white politicians who were running against blacks, Atlanta's blacks would vote for the white man. "It was a matter of practical politics," the Senator said repeatedly. "If a black man can't win an election and just runs for the hell of it, or to show some kind of protest, then I said let us vote for a liberal white man who can win." Of course, he was called Uncle Tom by some blacks.

Now Johnson went directly to Mayor Massell, and after a few preliminaries, threw his straight right to the chin. "I'd like to bring the Ali–Frazier fight here," he told Massell, who turned pale and seemed to be in shock according to Johnson.

"Leroy," the Mayor said after a very long pause, "I can't say no to you. Go ahead."

Leroy Johnson became part of the promotional group. In honor of Harry Pett, whose company's name was "House of Spice," Kassel and the Senator formed a promotional group with the name "House of Sports."

On August 11, this House of Sports conducted a formal meeting for the press after obtaining everyone's approval privately. At this meeting, Muhammad Ali was issued a permit to fight in Atlanta, and another permit allowing an Ali–Frazier fight to be conducted in the city on October 26. A four-hundred-dollar fee was granted for the leasing of the five-thousand-seat Municipal Auditorium.

After going through all these shenanigans, headaches, and tremendous difficulties, then, for the first time, the Frazier people were contacted. Yarcey Durham protested: "Nobody ever talked to us about money even."

The truth was that not knowing what was going on, and with so many false alarms in the past, Frazier had gone with his band to Las Vegas, and was very much out of shape. But the promoters already had an alternative: Jerry Quarry. House of Sports guaranteed Quarry one hundred and fifty thousand, Ali three hundred thousand. Quarry gladly accepted. Conrad, always working for the next promotion to go through, said to Senator Johnson when Frazier pulled out, "Why Quarry is even better than Frazier. Whitey's got to have someone to pull for, and Quarry, let's face it, is paler than Joe."

Now, Doctor Ralph Abernathy, Coretta King and other prestigious blacks from Georgia came in to help on the final struggle. "It was a black struggle," recalls the House of Sports publicist, Harold Conrad. "When Mrs. King went to Maddox looking for endorsement—although he didn't want to go through with it—there wasn't much he could do against it. The Attorney General had ruled that Ali had to be allowed to fight."

Conrad also told me that: "In the beginning, Maddox had accepted the fight and then had changed his mind.

"We agreed—more or less—we had an agreement," Conrad continued, "that he would have to make some remarks about the fight that he didn't want it here, but he knew there was nothing he could do about it. In the meantime, while we were training in Atlanta, the New York Supreme Court ruled that Ali must be given a license—and Ali was licensed also in New York."

House of Sports was skeptical about the real possibilities of the fight until about a week before it took place, although, of course, they went through all the motions. But they were having problems, which people never heard about, buried political problems, some of which may take years to reach the public surface. It was only two weeks before the match that the promotional group began to spend real money and it took until a week before the fight to invest the first hundred thousand dollars.

Ali remembers the Atlanta struggle very well. He didn't believe in the possibility of a fight either. He remembered telling Senator Johnson: "If I got a license in Atlanta, then let's get an exhibition first, and get me in with anybody in the ring and have a referee there, judges and officials there, then I think that'll be a historic moment, and this will prove that, most likely a fight could go through. Then I believe in a Quarry fight. But even a few days before the fight I figured something else might stop it, because money was involved."

Ali was wrong, however, and the fight took place, and made a fortune, as we know, for the people involved in its origins; a reward for the bold, and Atlanta had a night it will never forget. Ali went on to New York and Bonavena, and then on to preparations for the Frazier fight and the most enormous promotion in the history of boxing.

CHAPTER 15

The profession of fight promoter first came into prominence in 1910 when a saloonkeeper, Alaskan claim jumper and gambler "Tex" Rickard, offered a $101,000 purse for the upcoming struggle between Jack Johnson and the "White Hope" Jim Jeffries to be held on July 4, 1910, in Reno, Nevada.

Some sixty years later, a talent agent, and also a "gambler," offered Muhammad Ali and Joe Frazier the unprecedented sum of two-and-a-half million dollars *each* as a guarantee for their "Fight of the Century." Jerry Perenchio, then a well-known name only to a small group of cognoscenti who read *Variety* and knew he represented Glen Campbell, Andy Williams, Liz Taylor, Richard Burton, Jane Fonda and the Beatles, rocketed onto the sports scene with his offer.

Perenchio (called "Mr. Pinocchio" by one of the temporary secretaries hired by his New York Chartwell office) is a businessman who made his money in today's climates and by one of today's business rules: "use other people's money."

It wasn't his own money he pledged to Ali and Frazier. In fact, he almost didn't have any money to pledge. Not a boxing fan nor much of a sports fan, his only previous connection to sports being the swimming team in college, he became enchanted with boxing's potential after viewing the Ali–Quarry fight on closed-circuit TV in Los Angeles. Now, obsessed with the idea of promoting "The Fight"—as it was later to be labeled by Barney Nagler of *The Morning Telegraph*—he started calling potential backers. And he called, and called, and called, and marked off the names as more and more "money-men" turned down the opportunity to invest $5 million.

Far down on his list was the name of Jack Kent Cooke. Potential backer and active sportsman, Cooke's credentials read like the Encyclopedia of Sports: partial owner of the Washington Redskins football team, owner of the Los Angeles Lakers basketball team, owner of the Los Angeles Kings hockey team and owner of the Los Angeles Forum, indoor mecca of sports in America's third largest city. Cooke was, in the words of a gambler, a "natural."

Funded by Cooke's letter of credit (ironically, not one penny had to change hands for the guarantee, with a New York bank providing a letter of credit of $4,500,000 to the two participants, and the other $500,000 was put up by the Garden to insure the fight). Perenchio now started negotiating with the principals' managers.

But there were other bidders for the legendary confrontation of a boxer and a puncher. For a while it seemed that the Houston Astrodome would get the fight, because of its larger seating capacity—47,000 to the Garden's 21,000—and because Fred Hoffheinz, the Judge's son, had put together the closed-circuit telecast of the Bonavena–Ali fight. But showing their same allegiance not to the groups that had benefited them and stuck with them, but to the money that each group brought him, the Ali and Frazier camps listened to anyone bearing gifts.

First of all, Mike Malitz and his new group, Action Sports, which had put together the comeback of Ali, thought they had the fight when they put together a proposal and placed it on the desk of the Garden's matchmaker, Harry Markson, on the morning after the Bonavena fight. Hoffheinz was there with his presentation for the Astrodome and even Tommy O'Connor, the owner of a Philadelphia radio station and closed-circuit promoter, had a $5 million package for the two fighters. Both Malitz and Hoffheinz had figured all the total guarantee needed was $4 million. Since $5 million obviously had more of a ring than $4 million, Perenchio's offer was not only listened to, but encouraged by the management of Cloverlay and Ali.

On the 30th day of December, a notice was sent out to the press that "The Fight" would be announced at noon at the-then sports headquarters of New York, Toots Shor's. And at the exact hour of the announcement, as the press flocked into this momentous conference and newsmen jockeyed for position against the newsreel cameramen, Perenchio and Markson were all locked up working out the final details.

Now they came into Shor's, Ali talking from the moment he walked into the door, mouthing his pat phrases, "Now we'll see who the *real* Champ is," "If he whups me, I'll crawl across the ring and kiss his feet," "Look at me, I'm pretty, not a mark on me. When he fought Bonavena he fainted in the dressing room." Next came Frazier. Dressed smartly, he was a quiet contrast to the ebullient Ali. According to artist LeRoy Neiman, "Frazier is a flashy dresser. The power of his physique dominates his threads and you always feel you're looking at a powerful man rather than a well-dressed man." He took his place at the table next to New York Boxing Commissioner Ed Dooley, who somnolently tried first to keep the two apart and then to ignore them as if he was missing either his afternoon nap or the festivities still going on at the bar in the next room. While all of this intramural shoving was taking place at the table in front of the room, photographers, cameramen and reporters continued to shove each other and mouth profanities as they tried to get in on the history-making signing and announcement. In the midst of all this "excitement," a well-dressed man had entered the room, unnoticed by the crowd who had just begun to become acquainted with his name. Even if they knew this name, most men would not have been able to pronounce it.

His name was Perenchio. His manner was strong, almost manic, in a determined "I'm going to succeed, damn it" approach.

Rumors had it that Andy Williams had signed up the fighters and that Perenchio was just fronting for him, in much the same way he fronted for Williams and his other clients for his firm Chartwell (which he had also started on borrowed money).

But as they ascended the dais, it was soon clear who ran the show, and it was not Andy Williams, or Jack Kent Cooke or even the boisterous Ali. It was the determined Perenchio, who being interrupted by Ali's constant chattering while he was addressing the crowd, turned to him and said: "For $5 million, Ali, I think I have the right to talk, uninterrupted."

This man desired power, but anonymity. He wanted the front position, but not so much so that he and his beautiful wife Jackie were to become public figures. This might prove embarrassing to his representing those prima donnas who feel they are "talent." But his attitude was pierced by one of the deans of sportswriters, Milt Gross, who said, "If we want to know how many pubic hairs you have, we'll ask and know."

In the midst of his acknowledgement of questions by the reporters as to the accuracy of a *Wall Street Journal* article that morning that reported his ultimate windfall to be almost $40 million, Ali shouted to Frazier, "Joe, we've been had."

Well, maybe they hadn't been had, for their $2.5 million guarantee was the richest single payday in the history of sports, but it also provided a new dimension to the balance sheets of sports promoters. According to Perenchio he would "cut up and sell every part of the carcass, just like whaling."

Or so it seemed. Perenchio proposed to make the closed-circuit promoters put up one-half of their guarantee in advance cash, which if it came to pass, would mean that the local distributors would be bankrolling the entire promotion. If so, there would be more money in the bank than paid out by Perenchio and Chartwell, who had merely passed a letter of credit through the First National City Bank for their advance guarantee. It also meant the traditional fight promoters in many cities who had established their own local kingdoms would now be squeezed out by the big cash money available to movie men like Danny Kaye, or outfits like Concerts West, which put up the guarantees for the entire states of Washington, Oregon, Texas and California, or Loew's, which underwrote the rich territory of New York.

To Perenchio, it was merely an extension of his philosophy: "What we have here is the Mona Lisa. You expect us to sell it for chopped liver?" When people descend into boxing their elegance is quick to suffer.

He started plans for a program to be sold in each closed-circuit location for $2.00, complete with advertising. But no advertising was ever sold, although advertisers were apprised of its availability. Posters, that were a reprint of the cover showing both fighters in old-time boxing tights in the classic pose, were to sell at $1.00 each. And then there were to be commercials during the closed-circuit showing of the fight. These originally had been thought of as a $4 million package. The second-largest advertising agency in the world, McCann–Erickson, was approached to take the entire package and to parcel them up amongst their prestigious group of clients, Buick, Coca-Cola, Nabisco, Westinghouse, Esso, John Hancock and General Motors. When the president of McCann, Paul Foley, asked the obvious question, "What happens if this bout ends before the 15th round, and we don't get in all of the commercials?", he was greeted with a knowing nod and a statement that "Ali and Frazier are businessmen. They're too smart for that." So much for selling commercials!

But while Perenchio was experiencing some difficulties, the Garden was facing none. Tickets were sold out within days of the announcement of the fight. Priced at $150.00 for ringside seats, down to $75, $50, and $20, the tickets could have been priced at double the sum, but in the words of Harry Markson, "We didn't think we should gouge the public." Although $150 was high enough, scalpers soon stepped in and accelerated the prices to $750 and by fight night $1000 per ringside seat.

While he had been pointing toward a fight with Frazier ever since he was exiled, Ali now acted in a curious, self-assured manner. Seen by Floyd Patterson at a Bar Mitzvah in Miami on Superbowl Sunday, Ali was a fat 225 and not at all worried. He patted his stomach and murmured: "I'll get it off, soon."

But how soon? With the proclaimed "Fight of the Century" under two months away, Ali was still taking it easy, more convinced than ever that he was fated to win, and that he still had his fabled "Champion's Touch." He had seen his 15th round knockout of Bonavena as a sign and compared his efforts against the Argentine Bull with those of Frazier and was impressed with his own performance. Furthermore, he read the magazines and newspapers and when all but three writers at the luncheon at Shor's picked Frazier, he was sure it was another sign just as it had been when all picked Liston to "whup" him.

When asked whether Frazier had a chance, he retorted in the time-honored wisecrack, "Frazier's got two chances: slim and none."

PART III

CHAPTER 16

March 8, 1971: The day of the Ali–Frazier fight. In about two hours Ali will be in the ring and tangling with Joe Frazier. Even in the dressing room, the traditional precautions are tougher, the police many times more numerous. Yet as I make notes in my pad, this room is full of people. Worse, we are waiting for television cameras to come in now, and television sports broadcaster Howard Cosell is waiting for the engineers to start his interview.

Normally, I understand what a fighter feels when he's waiting for his zero hour to arrive. But each fighter has his own particular way of dealing with fear.

Floyd Patterson used to walk into dressing rooms, and as soon as he sat on the massage table, began to yawn. Minutes after taking his clothes off, he would fall asleep, and wouldn't wake up until the man from the Commission would wake him to get ready.

A good club fighter, Eddie Gavin, used to sit down, get up, sit down again. I usually walked into his dressing room making jokes, but nothing would make him laugh. I used to laugh because I knew what he was going through.

The dressing room is more than the silence before the storm; it is like the symptoms before the illness or—worst of all—like the last minutes in death row.

Certainly for middleweight contender, Wilbert "Skeeter" McClure, a dressing room was death row. And he was a prisoner who didn't fear anything but death. He was impossible. He was a good fighter but he never learned how to control fear. That was one lie he never learned.

My life in dressing rooms was not much different from the others. I felt what Floyd, Gavin and McClure felt. But no one would suspect. I hid my emotions pretty well.

My father, my brothers, and my friends were always allowed to come to my dressing room. And talking to them, kidding with them, saying how I was going to beat my opponent kept me pretty busy. Then, when they left and I was alone with my manager, my trainer and the special cop, my thoughts would go directly into the ring. And my heart would begin pumping faster, the muscles in my stomach would shake, my eyes studied the ceiling, my fingers moved without any conscious message. My stomach would begin to make funny sounds; it would feel as if the room were an oven. I would repeatedly urinate, and my trainer would wipe off my sweating body. When I thought my feelings were getting the best of me, I got up and began to shadowbox, usually thinking that the invisible man was not really a fantasy but the man I was fighting in minutes.

The first time I heard a Muhammad Ali dressing room story was when he was Cassius Clay and came to New York's Saint Nicholas Arena to fight Billy Daniels. Artist LeRoy Neiman went to visit him for the first time. Never had met him before.

"I was in the front row in the press section at St. Nick's and this guy from *TV Guide* came up and said: 'You got to see this kid in the dressing room. I've never seen anybody act like that.' I didn't know what to expect, and got in about ten minutes before the fight. There's this beautiful, kind of golden-looking kid sitting there—absolutely unmarked. And I said, 'I'm going to do a drawing of you because you've got something special.' After I finished the drawing, he said: 'Let me look at that. You sit there,' he said after studying it, 'and you look at me and just draw that one like that. Let me draw.'

"So, on the same drawing I did he took a pen and drew an airplane on there and drew his head—he drew himself to look like a white man, which is a very customary thing—and then he draws an automobile, a limousine. And then he put, 'Heavyweight Champ by 1963, 1964.'

"As he was finishing the drawing—he was just putting in the auto—this guy from the Commission comes into the dressing room (and says): 'into the ring, Clay, time to go . . .' and all that shit, the real movie-kind-of-thing. Clay said, 'Wait a minute, I'm not finished with this drawing.' So the guy goes back out—kind of irritated—and he comes back in almost immediately and says, "alright now, let's get going.' Clay signed it 'the next champ,' took the pen, put it back together and handed it to me, got up and walked out. And, you know, he wasn't that great that night."

Ali's behavior in the dressing room had nothing to do with his bad performance against Daniels, for this is the way that Ali always behaves in dressing rooms. He did anything to keep his mind distracted. Artist Neiman's presence was a tremendous relief for Ali that night. It would have been for me, too.

Now with Howard Cosell asking questions and Ali making fun of him and "revealing" to the closed-circuit audience the round in which Frazier was going to fall, Ali is not thinking about the fight. His mind is "busy" with many other things.

Of course, Angelo Dundee, who is nervous in a corner, tells Cosell to hurry up. "This man has to rest," Dundee says. "Let's finish with this shit."

Doctor Pacheco and Bundini Brown are in the dressing room. They don't like what's going on either. This place is full of people. It is an uncomfortable position for anyone who really cares about his fighter. But as usual, Ali is the boss. And Ali says, "Let's go on."

Now Ali throws a jab at me. I laugh. He smiles. "Did you know that I almost fought this boy here?" he says as he puts his hand over my head. "That's right. This small boy wanted to step in the same ring with me."

I now remember when Ali came to Puerto Rico to fight a three-round exhibition bout with Jimmy Ellis just to help my show. I was fighting heavyweight Tom McNeeley in an over-the-weight match.

He told my wife, "You better give this little boy here a lot of soul food so he can be heavier and make some money fighting me. Otherwise you both be in trouble."

Dundee was in Puerto Rico with Ali, but he was not Ali's companion. The man who followed Ali wherever he went was Herbert Muhammad, son of Black Muslim leader Elijah Muhammad. One night, my trainer, Johnny Manzanet, Herbert, Ali and two other Puerto Ricans went out looking for "foxes." This is Ali's word for girls. They began the search through the San Juan bars at ten this night. I was training and went to bed.

People in Puerto Rico were not much aware of Black Muslims; their only knowledge was what they read about Muhammad Ali. So, every time Herbert was introduced to any Puerto Rican, it was necessary to say "the Son of God." And he didn't complain.

People called Ali, "Ali Baba," or "Muhali," or "Alimoha." Nobody could pronounce his new name correctly. But in Puerto Rico Ali never got mad, as he did back in the states, when someone would call him Cassius or Clay; he simply took time to teach the Puerto Ricans how to pronounce his new name.

The morning after "fox" chasing, I was quietly having breakfast at the San Geronimo Hotel when in walks this beautiful girl. "Cheqüi," she yells, "where is Ali Baba and the Son of God?"

"What?"

"Don't play dumb. Where is Ali Clay, the champion?"

"Shhh."

"Don't give me that shit," she says in Spanish. "I want my money." She sat on a chair beside me. "If you don't lower your voice," I said, "I'm not going to help you. Tell me, what happened?"

"Well, they didn't pay and . . ."

"I don't mean that. I mean *what* happened."

She lowered her voice and began to tell me the whole story of the night before. I was on the floor, and even she laughed with me. One of the Puerto Ricans who had participated with her in "the program" walked in as I was sitting hysterically on the floor.

"You tell him the story," she said to the visitor. "Tell Cheqüi what happened last night."

"*You* tell him," the young man said.

"Well, they found me at around ten-thirty and they said they wanted beautiful girls. So we went to different bars and to some of the hotels, but they couldn't get anything. At about two in the morning I decided that I would take them all on. So we went to this place. You know," she said, "I'm a tough girl."

"You got to be kidding," I insisted.

"The champion was first," she said. "He was good. Not a *super hombre* in bed, but pretty good. Then came the Son of God. Wow! Was he big. He was some salami. Anyway, then I took on your trainer and then this guy here."

"Tell him who was the best," the visitor said.

"You. You, of course," said the girl.

I called upstairs and Herbert came down. He brought with him fifty dollars in cash that Ali sent the girl, and pulling out a checkbook and a pen, Herbert wrote out a check for another fifty. The girl began jumping with excitement and gave Herbert a kiss on the cheek. Then the girl thanked me and left.

That night Ali looked terrific in his three rounds with Ellis and I won a decision over McNeeley. About fifteen thousand people came to watch the program.

Early next morning I was having breakfast and the same girl came running to me. "What kind of fucking shit is this?" she asked in amazement. "I go to the bank to cash my check, and, you know what happened?" she said slowly. "This motherfucker is not the Son of God. He is the fucking devil. His check bounced. Is it possible that God didn't put money in the bank for his Son?"

I thought of recalling the story to Ali now, but I felt that the Puerto Rican incident had happened long ago and that maybe his way of thinking had changed. He was now happily married with three kids, and as funny as I thought the story, Ali might not take it with humor. But stories like this one are the right medicine for dressing rooms.

Cosell finished his interview and Dundee is asking everyone to leave the room. "I never wish luck to my friends," I tell Ali, "but you know what you have to do in that ring. Think at all times. Keep your cool." Ali smiles and winks an eye. "My friend," he says, his voice low, "you saw my secret prediction. The man is going to fall in six." With that, I left the room. Remaining with Ali is Doctor Pacheco, Bundini, Dundee, Ali's bodyguard, Youngblood, and the man from the Commission's office. Behind the door, inside the room is a special cop.

Ali is there now alone with his thoughts. If he has been lazy in training, he will think about it. If he made mistakes in the gym which he thought he couldn't help, he'll think about them. He is going to think about the days he didn't run, the days he didn't box, the times he drank too many soft drinks to cool off too quickly, the nights he went to bed late, the moments when he boxed only three rounds and was tired.

Then he will counter with all the good things he did in training. And he will say to himself that he is with Allah.

Strangely this morning, as Ali was walking out from the weigh-in ceremony, Burt Lancaster came to see him and read a poem he had written. I don't remember the exact words but it read in part: "If Ali is like in the old times, like when his name was Cassius Clay, he'll knock Frazier out. If not, Allah will do it for him."

Ali laughed approvingly and that worried me. How can a fighter approve of something like that?

I thought it was a sign of defeat. This "poem" was an extension of all the things that Ali has been saying which had impressed me as pessimistic and negative attitudes.

"If I lose," he said repeatedly, "I'll crawl to Frazier's corner and I will kiss his shoes, then I'll tell him: 'You are the Greatest.' " He also said that he was slower, because he was older. But that now he is punching harder. "I don't have the speed I had before, but I have the power," he said. I didn't like these estimates.

As I walk through the aisle from the dressing room toward the ringside section to say hello to my friends sitting there, I can hear the murmuring crowd (20,455) which paid a lot ($1,352,961)— both figures are records for an indoor bout.

And looking at the $150 seats I see more fur than I saw in the Miami Beach hotels. Reporters ask me for my opinion. I simply say, "Frazier by a knockout." Now, let me get to my seat. I'm really nervous.

Part of this crowd went through hell to get in. Even those with tickets had to wait as long as one hour to make the *entrance*. Among the thousands of people on the sidewalks surrounding the Garden I saw scalpers selling one hundred and fifty dollar tickets for seven hundred. As I was coming in, a woman was almost in tears. She had been giving her ticket to the doorman when a mysterious hand snapped it from her hand.

The doorman saw what had happened but couldn't do anything.

I was walking in with Bernadette Devlin, Jimmy Breslin and my friend, Norman Mailer, and suddenly Miss Devlin, with her small figure, disappeared from view. I've never seen her again. I remember her telling me that this was her first time at a fight. "But I want Muhammad Ali to win. He has to win. I'm going to root for him," she said emphasizing every word with the knock of her fist on the table. "He better win."

This crowd is not the type who will stop to argue on their way to their seats about the technicalities of boxing. This is a crowd that came with different ideas, the most important being to look at each other. These are the women who come to fights with extreme clothes, twelve-inch-above-the-knee skirts, blouses cut very low, front and back, astonishingly long, silky hair and five-inch heels. They are the ones who wait until the fight is most interesting to get up and with a very slow, firm, conspicuous step, walk by the ringside aisle with people clapping and whistling at them.

I don't think this crowd would stop to look at girls walking by. But I see these girls here tonight around the seventy-five-dollar seats.

I sit in the first promenade. It's supposed to be a "press seat." Down in the press rows in front of the ringside seats are six hundred photographers and reporters, many of whom have never even been here to help in less important fights. Beside me is Pete Hamill, who writes about New York more than any New York reporter, but he's not downstairs. He's fuming. It's personal, I'm certain. The Garden doesn't like Hamill. Several times he has said too much.

While Ali is back in the dressing room, deep in concentration I hope, his brother is in the ring right now. Rahaman Ali is not doing so well. It is about an hour before "The Fight of the Century," and Rahaman is getting killed. He's a decent young man, very puritanical and seldom smiles. He is three years younger than his brother Muhammad, but they started to box at the same time. One reason he may not smile is that he can't box. Some rumors have it that Rahaman was the force behind Muhammad's induction into the Black Muslim forces. Certainly, Rahaman became a Black Muslim before Muhammad.

I'm uneasy. I still think that Ali will not be able to take Frazier's pressure. Too bad. I'm hoping for a miracle. When Ali is involved, anything can happen. I hope so.

I had gone to Miami a few times and I saw Ali in training. I boxed with him one round during his training for this fight. I have an idea how he will look tonight.

In the midst of my thought I see Rahaman Ali at the edge of being knocked out in the ring. It is the last round and I think he has lost the fight. The bell. The fight is over. Announcer Johnny Addie is giving the decision. Rahaman's first defeat in seven professional fights. An unknown guy named Dan McAlinden is the victor. They will have to tell Ali what happened with his brother. It will have its effect.

If you ask me what the difference is between Rahaman and Muhammad as human beings or as fighters, I would answer with a Puerto Rican expression: "The difference is like the sky from the earth."

Rahaman is as devoted to the Black Muslims as a Cardinal is to the Catholics. Ali is as devoted to the Muslims as say, the Pope is to the Catholics. The Pope after all is a politician who has to be flexible for his religion. The Pope even visits Rumania, knowing it represents the technical opposite of what he represents. The Pope adjusts.

A Cardinal would be tougher. Like Rahaman. "José," he told me in Miami, with sincere passion, "I hate whites. They are no good. I don't even smile at them. I hate them. I hate them."

He doesn't go around the bushes and everyone knows it. He is like the fighter who learns to "follow the book by the letter," as we say in Puerto Rico.

I don't know the names of the fighters in the ring now, but I know that this is the semifinal. Ali's bout is after this one. Every seat is taken.

From my seat I can see Frank Sinatra with a camera and he is in the press row. A girl taps my back to show me former United States Vice President Hubert Humphrey, who is sitting a few rows to my left. In the balcony! It is a consolation! The semifinal is over. It won't be more than ten minutes before we see Frazier and Ali. I feel as if I'm the one to fight. I'm shaking with fear.

My mind travels to Miami again. Last trip I stayed in the same room with Bundini. We spoke about "The Fight." "He has to be right, if he wants to beat this guy," Bundini told me. "He's fuckin' around inside that ring. Too much fuckin' around." Ali is not taking training seriously. He doesn't have much respect for Frazier. He's running two and three miles instead of the customary five and six, and sparring in the gym has become more fun than business for "the champ."

Miami, I remember clearly, was Valhalla for the Ali entourage. That day Ali's parents were going to the Bahamas, and Bundini hadn't shown up in the gym. Youngblood was late, and Reggie, a young Black Muslim, who drove Ali around in Ali's Cadillac limousine, and kept the same hours as Ali, also arrived late.

With the except of Reggie, who would have converted me into a Black Muslim if I had spent more time with him, and of Dundee, who lives in Miami, Ali's entourage was having a continuous pre-victory celebration. You went to visit the rooms of Ali's "friends" and the most conspicuous product in the room— it was the result of their labors!—a couple of bottles of Scotch, soda and champagne.

Living it up . . . with Ali's money. And they always found female company to share "Ali's victory" with them.

That's past now. More important things are worrying Ali, and Dundee and Bundini. The Fight of the Century—biggest financial promotion in the history of boxing—is at the turn of the corner.

About now, the cops are on their way to tell Ali and Frazier that they should come out. Now is the point of no return. Are they scared!

Ali was not scared back in Miami, four weeks ago when he spoke in the Fifth Street Gymnasium. He ended that day's workout and told me: "José, come to my room later." Took a pen and a piece of paper and wrote his address down. "We are going to have fun tonight."

At seven we went in his limousine to pick up a friend at the airport. The show started.

Looking at one of the airport black employees, Ali yelled: "Hey you! Do you think you can beat me? Come on." And he pulled the guy toward him and began throwing punches over the head of the stranger. "I'll beat you up so bad." Then leaving the guy alone, Ali turned his head toward the crowd which began to form around him. "I aaam the baaadest nigger in America," he yelled. "I'm going to play with Frazier and then I'm gonna come back here to beat . . . you," he said, picking up a young black kid and then kissing him. "You," he continued, pointing to the same black kid, "are probably the young man who will grow up to beat me. No one older than you can or could ever beat me. I am the greatest."

Again, I was helplessly laughing. His remarks are funny no matter how many times he says them. "You know who that man is laughing on the floor?" he asks. "Hosey Torrays, the former light heavyweight king. He is almost as pretty as me. Almost."

At nine we left the airport to go to the Fountainbleau. We sat at a counter to have something to eat. Two minutes later Ali stood up saying he was coming right back. Meanwhile the rest of us ate.

Fifteen minutes later I walked toward the entrance of the hotel to see if I could see Ali. There he was. Hundreds of people surrounding him. "They don't let me move," he told me. "I don't know what I'm gonna do with my life." We both laughed and then he said to the excited crowd, "Please let me go, I have to eat, I have to get strong for 'Smokin' Joe.' "

As he began excusing himself for coming back so late, more people came toward us. As if hit by a bolt of lightning, he got up again and began yelling: "Here is the kiiiing. That's right. I'm the greatest heavyweight champion in the history of boxing. The prettiest, the fastest, the sweetest."

All heads turn toward him in seconds. People began crowding around us. Gladly he began signing autographs and talking with people. For fifteen minutes he simply enjoyed himself with what he loves the most; the admiring looks of people, a lot of them.

As usual he entertained. "Anyone who don't like it can get outside with me."

"Let's go," he ordered after the game which the admirers played out.

We hopped into the limousine and the chauffeur asked, "Where?"

"Newport," answered the champ. "We're gonna see the Treniers. They're my men."

The car threaded slowly along Washington Avenue and we headed north for about twenty minutes. Ali, dressed in black trousers and a long-sleeve black shirt that he refused to put inside his pants, got out of the car and walked downstairs to the club in the fancy Newport Hotel.

Now he remained quiet for a few moments. A show was going on. Some of the black men who belonged to the Treniers group passed by and Ali spoke to them.

Later he sat in the club to wait for his friends to begin the show. For a few minutes we watched the Treniers in action and Ali applauded. Then one of the Treniers acknowledged the presence of Ali.

"We'd like to tell you that we have with us tonight a great man. The heavyweight champion of the world, Muhammad Ali," said Claude Trenier.

Claude's identical twin, Heathcliff, started to kid around. "Well, he said, "Ali's here, but he's gonna be in trouble with tough Joe Frazier. Man, he is in trouble."

"No, man," said Claude, "Ali is the greatest."

"Not for long," continued Heathcliff. Ali was watching carefully from his seat. "Are you crazy?" screamed Ali from his seat.

"You-are-in-trouble," said Heathcliff putting his hand to his head, which he rocked from side to side.

"You are black, but you are dumb," shouted Ali. Then Ali whispered to me, "Make believe you're holding me back." Now Ali pretended to be struggling to get away from me. "C'mon, José, let me go," he yelled, "I'll knock this bum out."

Grimacing at Heathcliff, he shouted, "Frazier is mine in nine, but if you keep up the jive, you'll go in five." *Mucho* menace.

I let him go and Ali dashed toward the stage making animal sounds and yelling unintelligibly. The pianist grabbed Ali. "Don't hurt my man," he pleaded.

"He's the one gonna get hurt," yelled Heathcliff at Ali, while brother Claude pretended to hold him back.

"You know," Ali said, "you look like your brother and you even sing like him, but you surely are not smart like him. Man, you're *dumb*."

The audience went wild with laughter. "I have one last word for you," Ali said into the microphone. "I am a *baaad* nigger."

He walked off the stage to wild applause.

The show ended and we began to leave when a white-haired man dressed in a white suit made a comment of which we could only hear the last word, "Frazier."

"What did you say?" Ali asked, half shouting.

The man was not intimidated. "I said that Frazier will knock your brains out," said the man.

Again Ali told me to hold him back. "You wanna fight me? I'm going to knock you out, you loudmouth," Ali had found his greatest insult. "Let me go, José, I'm going to hurt this phony."

The man's wife was in a panic. She thought the scene was real. The white-haired middle-aged man thought so, too. "I'll fight him," said the man who seemed to have had one too many. "C'mon," he pleaded with his wife, "Let me go and fight him."

This went on for a few minutes until Ali, afraid that the man's wife could have a heart attack, decided to leave. They saw us as we were getting into Ali's limousine. The windows up, Ali pretended he was still yelling at the man. In fact he was simply moving his lips silently while gesturing wildly with his arms.

On the road, a few minutes later, we noticed a Cadillac come up beside us, and we saw the white-haired man again. Ali opened the door of his car while going sixty miles an hour. "You want trouble?" he yelled from the rear seat. "Stop the car, you bum. Stop the car," he yelled out.

Both cars stopped for a red light. Ali got out and made believe he was trying to open the guy's car door. The woman inside looked terrified.

But when the light changed and Ali got back into his car he was laughing.

And he was seen laughing by the passengers of the other car. Now we could see an attitude of relaxation come into their faces. The white-haired man driving the car, rolled down the window. It was 2 A.M. "Hey," he shouted. "Let's have breakfast together."

"You see," Ali said to us in the car. "This man hated me before tonight. He wanted to see Frazier win this fight. But now he has changed. I have given him more than half an hour of my time and he is very excited about it."

We all got out at Wolfie's Delicatessen and the white-haired man rushed toward Ali. "Man, you're great," he said.

The white-haired man's wife grabbed one of Ali's arms and began pulling him toward Wolfie's. The white-haired man embraced Ali, saying, "I swear to God I'm going to New York to see the fight." Then as if he were with his own son, the white-haired man planted a kiss on Ali's cheek. He was a big shot and he was in a rich man's heaven.

I'm looking around to see if I see the white-haired man sitting in the ringside seats but I can't see him. I'm sure he is here tonight. He must have been about sixty. Ali's treatment surely extended his life. He *has* to be here now.

Noise. People stand up. Not a soul is on his seat. One of the fighters is coming out. He's throwing punches to the air. He is wearing white with red stripes and a mini-robe.

Commotion!

Muhammad Ali!

It is him! And he is smiling and waving at people he recognizes in the crowd. Ali is behaving as if this fight is not special. Yet Ali is stepping into the ring under the wildest welcome ever given to a pugilist. Blacks are going crazy. He is the real champ.

As soon as he gets in the ring, he's walking around with his arms up in the air. Now he does the "Ali Shuffle"—I think of Cus D'Amato, sixty years old, hitting him while he does the Ali Shuffle—the crowd goes wild. Right now Ali is the literal center of the show, the nucleus of the crowd. Just yesterday he had said to me: "I wouldn't enjoy these fights half as much if I wasn't able to see what's happening." That's a remark! Ali is still a spectator to the events he creates. He's playing both parts. Ali is showing off to *his* crowd; Ali is showing the *other* crowd, the ones who hate his face, how beautiful he is.

You cannot see Ali frightened. He has mastered those feelings. He is going to use them to beat Frazier.

As the crowd gets ready to sit down, Joe Frazier comes out. He is also throwing punches, but he's looking down, he is not watching the crowd. He listens to them. He is getting a tremendous cheer. Judging by the crowd's reaction, both fighters are equally liked. Trainer Yancey Durham is with his man.

Frazier is wearing a fancy outfit: velvet brocade, green and gold trunks with matching robe. He has white shoes. I think he looks ridiculous. He steps into the ring. Looks mighty strong.

Ali talks with Bundini. Now he leaves Bundini and moves around. He is moving toward Frazier. He pushes Frazier with his shoulder. Ali is using his psychic powers. Frazier smiles at him. Ali pushes him again. This time Frazier grins. They both smile now. Both look resigned. The fight is finally going to be on. Ali stops. He probably realizes that he's relaxing Frazier who seems to play his part well.

All the pre-fight antics are over. The name calling is over, over as far as the public is concerned. For when this fight starts, there is going to be some name calling inside the ring.

The autonomous Negro, as Eldridge Cleaver called Ali in his book *Soul on Ice*, is fighting the subordinate Negro. Ali's tactic had been to make Frazier, who is darker than Ali, "The White Hope." "He calls me Uncle Tom," Frazier said once, "and I call him a phony." And many people are here to see the White Hope destroy the nigger.

It is not the first time that this has happened. In Maine, when Ali knocked out Sonny Liston in their second encounter, I heard a young white man screaming at Liston: "Smash that nigger's mouth. Kill the nigger," not bothering to look at Liston who was considerably blacker than Ali.

Ali has that power. He changes people. He blinds people. Many times you see what Ali wants you to see and not what is there. "If Ali says that he is going to walk on the East River," Garden matchmaker Teddy Brenner said yesterday, "you can bet your ass that over one hundred thousand people will be there to see if it's true." In fact, Brenner had picked Ali because Ali said he was going to play with Frazier.

Arthur Mercante is the referee for this match. He is one of the best in the business. In fact, he is one of the few referees who trains consistently to keep himself in shape. I like him because he lets fighters fight inside. And in-fighting, I think, is an art. But tonight I hope he doesn't let the fighters stay inside too long. If that happens, Ali could get killed. Ali can't fight inside. Frazier is an in-fighter.

As announcer Johnnie Addie makes the announcement, the crowd remains quiet. They burst into wild applause only when the names of the fighters are announced.

I'm thinking about Ali's last poem about Joe. "They call Joe Frazier *Smokin' Joe* because he talks about he's hot," Ali said yesterday. "He always talks about he's gonna come out smoking. So I wrote a poem and it describes what happens."

> Joe's gonna come out smoking
> And I ain't gonna be joking,
> I'll be pecking and a-poking
> Pouring water on his smoking.
> This might shock and amaze ya,
> But, I'm gonna re-tire Joe Frazier.

At the New Yorker Hotel, where I had a long talk with Ali yesterday, he gave me a smart and sensible answer when I asked him why he was so sure Frazier would be no-contest. "He doesn't have the ability or speed of Floyd, the punching power of Liston or Cleveland Williams, the awkwardness of Bonavena or Miltonberger (Mildenberger), so," he finished with his ironic smile, "since we can't get along, we're going to fight along."

He had been in his usual nice mood. I don't know if he knew, but I had picked Frazier to beat him in my last Saturday column in the *Post* and in *Boxing Illustrated*. In fact, I had made an imaginary account of how the fight was going to go. It was my honest opinion and I always felt that Ali respected honesty. But just before I went up to see him in his room, my friend Budd Schulberg told me that Ali's people were mad at me, meaning Dundee, Pacheco, Bundini and Youngblood. I couldn't understand why, but I think Pacheco told Budd that Ali was not, but they were. The doctor told Budd that they felt Ali had some respect for me and that my column could affect him psychologically. I had agreed with that. I was hating myself.

Sincerely, I wanted to be wrong. I had stated my opinion based on my knowledge and experience in what I thought I did best. Maybe that's why Schulberg just bet on Ali. He sees boxing one way, I see it another.

After a while people started to come in and Ali became the fighter again. He started to yell, "I am the greatest. I am the greatest." Then he began to watch television, full of special programs about the fight.

We watched the first Frazier–Bonavena match, when Oscar hit Frazier and Frazier went down. "Can't fight," screamed Ali.

Later on, the set showed how Frazier was beating Chuvalo. "Do you think I'll do that?" Ali asked of no one in particular. "Do you think I'm going to stay in one spot that long?" He answered himself. "No sir. That man is not going to get me to stand still for more than five seconds."

I told him I had to go and he shook my hand. I saw his smile again, that ironic smile, which was ready to talk.

Supernormally, he still has that smile now in the ring. I don't know what they are saying to each other, but I see their lips moving. The battle they are having now is who can deceive the other. They both know that the other is next to paralyzed. They should know. It is very possible that what they say to each other here now, might have some relevancy to the result. One *can* be a victim of a temporary trauma. A forty-five minute trauma.

I remember, when I fought Pastrano for the championship (Dundee was in his corner), the Garden, after days of negotiation, agreed to play the Puerto Rican National Anthem. My trainer was in front of me and I asked him to move out. I wanted Pastrano to see me singing the anthem with that large Puerto Rican crowd. My throat was tight but after a few bars it loosened up and I hit the notes on pitch and my voice was good. I could feel Pastrano's reaction. "If that mother can sing at a time like this, he's going to be killing me in two minutes."

When Willie came out in the first round and threw his favorite weapon—a jab—I countered with my own. He shook his head with repugnance. When I walked back to my trainer Johnny Manzanet, after the first round, I said: "Johnny, he's mine." Johnny said, matter-of-factly: "Since the anthem." And then he said, "Shhh!" And slapped my face nervously to keep me from talking.

Ali and Frazier have just been instructed by Arthur Mercante. In thirty seconds we are going to see the first round of The Fight of the Century. I'm just thinking about what Yancey Durham said before the fight. He had sounded cool. "The first round is going to be Ali moving away with my man chasing. Clay is going to look good," Durham said. "In the second, Clay is going to be like in the first, moving fast and Joe missing. In the third, Clay is going to start getting hit in the body. By the sixth he might start picking the place where he's going to fall. He shouldn't be able to take Joe's punishment for more than seven rounds." Durham is not a man who is known to brag about his fighter, but this prediction sounded accurate enough for me. My idea of the fight was more or less the same.

Dundee put it this way: "It's a very dangerous fight. Tough fight. This will be a great fight. Muhammad's toughest fight. But he'll beat Frazier! Frazier is made-to-order for him. I love that kind of style for him. I feel Joe Frazier's fighting a fighter he won't be able to contend with. This guy's got the speed, the agility. He's going to make him fall short with punches. Frazier's never missed people with punches before cause guys were there to be hit. This guy is not gonna be there to be hit and he, Frazier, is gonna catch punches. And if Joe walks into a shot—leaping at Ali or trying to catch him—he's gonna get nailed. It could be the end of the fight.

"If Ali plays with him I'll not be surprised. I won't be surprised at anything this guy does."

Dundee had told me that about three weeks ago. But in Miami about a week before this night, I asked Dundee, Cassius Clay, Sr., and Bundini the same question: "Why do you think Ali is going to win?"

"This man is destined to be the greatest," was Dundee's response.

"Champions are born, they are not made," Clay, Sr. answered proudly. Could any father say the opposite?

"God is his trainer, his manager, his companion. God and only Him, will win this fight," Bundini said with conviction—he was part of the Trinity.

You can't go to a boxing man like myself and offer that kind of explanation. They knew it. If they were expecting Ali to win by something based on those answers, then it would be proper to think that they were whistling scared.

That afternoon Ali had not been too good. In fact, he had been hit with some good shots from three of his sparring mates.

I, myself, had boxed that day with Ali. In the one round I sparred he took it easy. He knew this was my first time with boxing gloves in two years. It was only after the first two minutes that Ali began to use a little pressure on me. He threw a few combinations and I made him miss. At one point he lay against the ropes and I hit him with a couple of hard shots to the body. There was a moment when I used a double right hand—uppercut to the body and short right to the head—and both punches made contact with the spots I had chosen. But I had to admit Ali was fantastically fast with both his hands and legs.

Yet, again, what really worried me was his head. Physically speaking, I couldn't make any judgment on the one round we boxed. I made other judgments after I saw him finishing his training with the other sparring partners. I came to the conclusion that Ali's reclining back against the ropes was no theater, no tactic, no laziness. It was a habit. A habit created by the sensibility he developed in the three-and-a-half years he was off.

It took three-and-a-half years to develop that habit, and he's not going to break it in one night. One conclusion I have and it is what Cus told me a few minutes ago: "I think both of them (Ali and Frazier) lost some interest in boxing. They are saying that they are going to quit after this one. If they are telling the truth then it means that they have lost some desire to fight. So we might be seeing a lousy fight tonight."

But it has been established. A fighter lies a lot. When Ali and Frazier said that they might quit, they could very well be lying. One thing is sure. Ali is going to lay back against the ropes and he might run into damaging hooks.

The assumptions are over. The crowd is silent. The fighters are ready to charge at each other. In the corner, Ali just ended his prayer. It seems as if the man with the bell can't start this damn fight.

The echo just reached me. The bell.

CHAPTER 17

Frazier walks straight in, Ali comes in a circle. They both meet almost in the center of the ring with Ali feinting. Frazier charges, slower than a tank, faster than the fastest turtle. He is like a special machine, a computerized machine which has been fed only with a truth chart. A machine which will reject lies automatically. You can't lie to this machine. You can't fool him with your feints. The first thing Ali does is to try.

Ali jabs. He jabs again. Frazier bobs and weaves as he comes in to Ali. Now Frazier falls short with his own jab. Ali steps back and counters with a jab. Frazier still walks in. Ali stops and throws a jab, another jab. A lot of his punches are missing. Steps back. Frazier keeps coming. Ali stops again, he throws a jab, steps back, feints, throws a fast jab and follows with a right cross, comes back with a fast left hook–right cross combination. A lot of his punches are still missing. Frazier still charges.

Joe is moving his head as he comes in. His body moves from side-to-side, his strong legs push him in, his hands move up and down, his chin close to his chest. He jabs and hits Ali on the gloves. Ali moves back. Frazier connects for the first time in the fight. It is a right to Ali's chest. Ali keeps moving. He moves straight back and Frazier follows. It is a relentless pressure. Ali looks cool as he moves back with class, looks like the old Ali, the young Cassius Clay. Ali hits Frazier with a jab, steps back and throws a slow chop of a right which goes over Frazier's head.

Frazier keeps the same pace. They are inside now and Ali pushes Joe to the side and hits him with a jab. Ali smiles. Frazier throws a left that falls short again. The bell. Ali's round.

Ali is good tonight. Pete agrees. The first round was not what you call a one-sided round for Ali, but undoubtedly he won it.

As the crowd sits quietly waiting for the second round, I see Ali standing in his corner. He didn't sit down after the bell. He's still trying to lie. He hasn't understood yet that you can't lie to a machine. But Ali looks confident. He looks as if he is going to be a hard man to knock out tonight. If he keeps up that confidence I see in his eyes, he'll play with Frazier. He seems to be listening to what Dundee is telling him. The bell.

Again Ali comes in a circle. Again, he feints. Frazier jumps back and jumps back in. Frazier seems to be in the path of Ali's punches while at the same time he doesn't seem to be able to reach Ali. It's understandable. Ali's reach is eighty-two inches to Frazier's seventy-three and-a-half. Besides, Frazier has been trained to use his shoulders and body with his punches. He has to come close to you to land solid blows. In turn Ali taught himself to use only the snap of the arms. So, he doesn't have to be too close when punching.

Ali stops now. He throws a barrage of punches. Pushes Frazier back beautifully and then jabs at him again. Ali smiles again. He had Frazier on defense a second ago. Now Ali moves with Frazier chasing, maintaining the same exact pace. Ali's eyes seem to be fixed on Frazier's forehead. Frazier's on Ali's chest. Fighters have subconscious habits. Some believe that the opponent's eyes send them a message before a punch comes. Others feel that looking at the opponent's gloves gives them the clue. I always looked at my rival's chest. Nobody taught me, but I felt that something moved around the other man's chest muscles before the punch came out.

Ali circles around Frazier and looks like he has never been away from a ring. Jabs come out like old times. He jabs again, moves to his right, now to his left. Frazier follows. His face seems like a wild animal. He looks like he's grunting as he keeps up his chase. Like Bonavena, Frazier is waiting.

Ali jabs and Frazier falls short again. The truth is that Ali is not moving voluntarily, he's being forced to move. It reminds me of what Joe said yesterday: "It is not the same when a fighter moves because he *wants* to move, and another when he moves because he *has* to." But again, Frazier is not cutting the ring short, he is following Ali.

Frazier connects this time with a jab to Ali's head. Another jab by Frazier falls short. Ali comes back with a jab of his own that passes over Frazier's moving head. Another jab by Ali that misses. Frazier seems to put a little more speed to his charges. Twenty seconds to go and Ali throws a left–right combination, both over a moving target. They get close, and there is the bell.

This round could be considered one-sided. But what caught my eye here is that Ali won the first two minutes and forty seconds handily, but for the last twenty seconds he did nothing while Frazier seemed to increase the pressure.

Again, Ali stands up in his corner. Frazier sits down to listen to Durham who speaks calmly to Joe. Dundee is doing the talking in the opposite corner. Once in a while Bundini says something. But when Dundee opens his mouth, Bundini remains quiet. Another corner man with Frazier washes his mouthpiece. Durham wipes some of Joe's sweat from his forehead.

Ali remains with his mouthpiece in his mouth. I don't know why. It is a relief—or it was for me—to have that bulk out of my mouth. But Ali might have his own reasons. After all, who has his mouth?

Third round. Frazier gets up as usual. He walks straight to Ali who has to meet him in his own corner. Ali doesn't circle around as he did in the first two rounds. Ali moves one, two, three steps back into the ropes. There he is! Against the ropes! Is he tired already? Frazier begins to work. A wild left by Frazier. Ali pulls back and the hook sends waves of hot air to ringsiders. It went so fast you couldn't see the glove. It was a hard, very hard left hook. Ali remains on the ropes. Joe looks for openings. Joe connects with a right to the body, comes back with another long left hook, it misses again. Ali still against the ropes. Joe hits with a vicious left hook to Ali's elbow. A right that hits Ali's face as it moves away. A fast hook grazes Ali on the right side of his face. Now Ali tries to move, Frazier won't let him. Joe pushes Ali back to the ropes. Ali smiles. Now Frazier smiles.

Another hook by Frazier lands on Ali's face, but without any power. Ali saw it coming and rolled with the punch. Ali gets out. Frazier pursues with anger. He chews his mouthpiece. Ali flicks a jab. Another one. Joe is walking now like a German tank. Yes, it is a machine with brains. Frazier only stops when he has Ali against the ropes. His legs cease to move. The switch that turns the movement of the legs off, automatically puts the hands on. And that's happening now.

Frazier throws vicious punches. Ali looks at the crowd and shakes his head no. He is not hurt. His constituents laugh. Ali now smiles at the crowd. Again, his crowd laughs and applauds. Meanwhile, Joe is punching. Joe punches now to Ali's stomach. Joe furiously throws a left hook, a right, another hook. Only the right made contact. Frazier is making the fight.

Ali throws a flurry of punches which wouldn't budge my sister. Now Frazier is the one who laughs. The "other crowd" laughs with him. He has his constituency here too. Frazier comes back. A mean left hook misses Ali by accident. Ali never saw that punch. He was moving at the time Joe happened to throw it. Somehow Ali has not been hit with a real damaging blow. He seems to hold some control over his thinking. His head is clear. He knows what's going on. Is he testing Joe's punching power? Is he trying to get Joe to punch himself out? Is he being stupid? Is he trying to discourage Joe? These questions seem to be in everybody's minds. But the question to ask is: Can he do otherwise? Is this put-on, or real?

My question is: Is he lying again?

Muhammad Ali is too smart to stay against the ropes using that as a tactic. He's getting killed. Not in the literal sense, because Joe hasn't been hitting accurately, but Ali is losing this round big.

Ali doesn't even try to get off the ropes. He is in bad trouble if he keeps this up. You can't do that against a powerful man like Frazier. He has the power and the head that goes with it. Frazier is going to find an opening sooner or later. He isn't Bonavena who just throws punches at you. Frazier knows when to throw them.

Like now, he just hit Ali with a left to the body. Ali rolls with a left hook and a right-cross. The bell. This is a big round for Frazier. Perhaps, the worst round of the two hundred and four rounds Ali has boxed in his whole pro career, including the times when he was knocked down by Sonny Banks and Henry Cooper. In those fights he got up to finish the round on his feet. And lost those rounds in which he got knocked down only because of the punch that put him down. But here tonight, Ali was punished thoroughly and miserably for three full minutes. Sure, he didn't get hurt, but no one soul could say that *maybe* he won this round. And only a few here knew what effect those body blows might have later on. He just managed to lose this round big. I don't know what this might do to his confidence.

The bell just sounded for the start of the fourth round.

Frazier comes out fast toward Ali who tries to move but can't. Ali is caged again against the ropes. What is he doing? Ali laughs with the crowd. He's lying. He's been too obvious.

The pattern of the fight changed in the third round and it seems as if this new pattern will prevail for the next couple of rounds. Of course, this transition is being forced by Frazier on Muhammad, who tried to establish a pattern in the first two rounds. And couldn't. Usually, the model of a fight is "mutually" agreed upon by both fighters. One of them chases, the other moves back. If the one in continuous motion and retreat, stops and finds out that by moving less he can hit his opponent and at the same time doesn't get hit *more* than he was when he was moving, then it would be *convenient* for him to slow his foot-work. It would, because he won't be "wasting" energy. If the pursuer feels that he's also now more comfortable hitting the other man, then the shift in pattern has been agreeable to both.

So here, Muhammad is installed against the ropes and Frazier is banging away with murderous punches. Naturally, he's not landing with half of them. This transition was chosen by Ali but it has been happily accepted by Frazier too. After all, wasn't he looking for this change? The trouble with Muhammad is that he is not sure of what he's doing. So in between he shakes his head, woos the audience, sticks his tongue out at Frazier, smiles and throws slaps at Joe.

If what he's doing in the ring is not giving him much pain now, you can bet it will when he sees the scorecards of the fight judges after the fight. He is alienating them. Ali is contributing to their natural prejudices. Don't forget, in the Ali–Bonavena fight the money man was Ali. Now he is not the future money man. He's not as far as Madison Square Garden is concerned. Frazier, we should remember, became champion in this town. And of his seven title defenses, including this one, four have been in New York. He is the clubhouse boy. Ali is the independent, the uncontrollable one. Ali has to win his fight. He knows that. Or at least he should know that if he fights a doubtful fight, the benefit of the doubt will probably go to his opponent.

In the ring he's still in the new pattern. He's "resting" in corners. The bell catches him for the second consecutive time on the ropes.

Ali walks slowly to the corner and for the first time in the fight, there is the stool waiting for him. He sits down. In the opposite corner Frazier sees Ali on the stool. Dundee is literally yelling at Ali. Dundee is talking and working on Ali's legs. He massages Ali's legs and Ali is saying something to him. If Ali once criticized football players, skiers, hockey players and even wrestlers for working in sports which were too dangerous, I don't know what he is thinking now. He once said: "I became a fighter because I didn't want to be hurt like in those other sports."

I hear the bell for the fifth.

Frazier flies toward Ali, who again chooses to stay in his own corner. Referee Mercante is letting the fighters stay inside. Mercante is doing a fine job. A referee should step in between the fighters only when one of them is holding with one hand and hitting with the other, when one fighter doesn't have the free movement of both hands, or when they are both inside doing nothing for a reasonable period of time. So Mercante does not make them quit the ropes. And Ali doesn't grab, he simply lays back on the ropes and evades some punches, takes some on his arms, some on the belly, a few on the face. He is not countering.

Patterns have to do with this matter. Muhammad changed his pattern from moving fast to seeking the ropes for more than one reason, the most important being that Frazier set up the change. Joe tried from the beginning to stop Ali from moving, to make him change his first pattern. Ali didn't for the first two rounds because he was fresh enough to move around without jeopardizing his future energy this night. He was hoping his speed would force Frazier to decrease his pressure. That way Ali could control the pace for the entire fight, and so run it on his best estimate of his *own* energy.

When the opposite occurred, and Ali was forced to take up Frazier's preference for a slower fight along the ropes, his professionalism panicked. You didn't see it. I saw it. He was not laying back against the ropes thinking that he was going to remain there all night because it was best for him. He was instead going to look for spots to let go punches like the one that toppled Bonavena.

In fact, he just tried to do that. Now, quickly, he moves out of the ropes and throws a stiff left jab. Feints. Goes back to the ropes and Frazier hasn't shifted tempo. So Ali connects, moves out, and comes back with a very fast left hook–right uppercut combination. The bell sounds with Ali's right on Frazier's nose. But Ali started too late. I think he lost this round too.

When pressure makes a fighter think ahead of time which precautions he should take, he is in trouble. Boxing is not a sport in which you can take an hour, a minute or a second to think. In boxing your sense of anticipation turns on *only* one-thousandth of a second before the actual action.

When a man is losing a match and then tries to change the pattern, he could be doing one of two things: searching to turn the tide—desperately—or looking for his excuse to lose a fight. However, when a winning fighter changes his pattern, the reasoning becomes more interesting.

For example, when I fought Pastrano, I knew that his best offensive weapon was the jab—he had a beautiful jab which came out of a deceptive movement—it was hard to anticipate; his best defensive weapon was his legs—they were very nimble. So, in the first round I outjabbed him, looking to beat him at his own game. In the second, I cut the ring short. It was some of the best fighting I had ever done, and it meant I had succeeded in lifting his best tools. In the third, I changed the pattern. After destroying his blueprint, I began using mine. I began to walk in and use my combinations to his body.

Ali, himself, did this when he boxed Cleveland Williams. After moving like lightning in the first couple of rounds in his own style, Ali came out in the third and outpunched Williams, and beat him at his own game—punching out murder. So he kept his body close to Williams in the third until his punches split the senses of the big man from Houston.

There are about thirty seconds left in this round, and for the last minute, Ali has been moving a little more than he did in the last few rounds. He hits Frazier coming in. Frazier misses a hook and a right cross, while Ali moves backward toward the ropes. Frazier smiles. The bell. Not too good, but not that bad. I can just about give this round to Ali. I am prejudiced in his favor but no more prejudiced than any judge who is subconsciously for or against him.

Ali sits on the stool and from here I can see how hard he's breathing. Both Bundini and Dundee are talking to him. In the other corner Frazier is also breathing hard. I think that Frazier has never been hit so much in his pro career. Both fighters are working under tremendous pressure.

In the sixth, Ali seems to move more. Jabs and moves. Jabs again. Frazier hasn't changed. He's still coming in. He wants to maintain himself like a mirror in front of Ali. Frazier wants Ali to think that his forceful body is Ali's double. Ali throws an uppercut. Misses. Ali is trying more. This is his third pattern. He begins to throw uppercuts to a head that doesn't stop moving.

No one can argue about these two men's class. Both have their own special class. Ali and Frazier both have learned every punch there is in boxing. Yet Ali seems to have a more likeable style. He seems to throw punches with a special elegance. Frazier throws punches like the word "boxing" sounds.

Could it be that Ali, with this elegance is working a premeditated plan in which he will show Frazier that he is not going to collapse in the later rounds under Joe's body attack, but can take it and to some degree give it back, and take it, and—here comes the doubt for Frazier—still be in there fighting about the time Frazier wears down? If this is true, he is indoctrinating Joe. Yes, Ali could be showing Joe that he can take anything Joe has to offer and come back later to give it back.

Ali is not doing too bad now. I look at the clock on the Garden's wall and see that there are only ten seconds left in this round. Ali remains against the ropes, but Joe doesn't have the same drive. Joe misses a left hook. Ali jabs from the ropes. Ali smiles at Frazier. Frazier smiles at Ali. Joe attacks and misses two wild left hooks, both to Ali's face. The bell. I'm trying to be as objective as I can, but I saw Ali winning this round. On my scorecard I have Ali ahead at the end of seven rounds, four rounds to three.

Still, it is not a great performance by either of the fighters. Ali and Frazier are giving us their best, but their best tonight is not the best of them. They are both better fighters than they are showing.

Frazier, the more impersonal of the two, is showing the effect of pre-fight pressure. Of course, the build-up of this fight had no parallel. Frazier, as objective as he looks, as impersonal and unemotional as he has shown himself to be, seems, all the same, trying to overdo it. He is forcing himself to do his best. He is not fighting his natural fight. Although he won rounds three and four handily, he doesn't have the zip he did in those two rounds.

Ali, at times, seems to believe what reporters have said about him: that his three-and-a-half years of inactivity have affected his performance, that he has lost speed of hands and legs, that he is pulling away from punches too slowly and that he's going to get caught with one of Frazier's powerful left hooks. It has to be a clash in his mind. I think he has come to believe reporters since the Quarry fight. So now his mind seems to be receiving no respect from his physical mechanism. The mind commands him to do this and the body is not answering. I only hope he can wake up. As long as the body can't believe what the mind says it can do, Ali will have trouble winning this match.

Round eight began thirty seconds ago. Ali walked out very slowly. Frazier goes straight to him, daring Ali, inviting him to try. "C'mon, phony, hit me if you can," Frazier seems to say. Ali has no expression on his unmarked face. Frazier is the first one to punch; a left hook to Ali who turns his body as the hook lands right above his right hip.

Both fighters, because of the special circumstances, might be worried about going the full fifteen rounds at this speed. Right at this moment the fight is halfway through. The punches that are making contact on Ali's body and head are not too damaging, or hard enough to produce a knockout. In return, Ali's punches, although they have brought a little blood to Frazier's nose and mouth, are not of any knockout caliber either.

My confusion here is that this fight is so close that I can't predict at this moment who I think is going to win. Ali is now against the ropes on the south side of the Garden and Frazier is throwing punches while people are screaming with excitement. Yet Ali is laughing.

I counted seven punches thrown by Frazier; seven punches missed the target. Ali drops his hands at times, daring Joe to hit him. Now, again, as in the fifth, Frazier drops his hands and Ali throws a one–two combination that hits Frazier flush on the face, above the jaw. Now Frazier is the one laughing. He laughs in Ali's face, and Ali is not laughing. Frazier's legs push him toward Ali and Ali goes back to his favorite spot tonight: the ropes. Frazier lashes out another of his attacks. They seem ineffective and, in fact, they are now, but they might have their effect later.

Ali should know by now that Joe is not being indoctrinated yet. At times he seems to forget and his legs carry him to the ropes, as if still tempting Joe. But Frazier always appears delighted by the invitation. Round eight ends. Frazier made this round.

Ali is welcomed in his corner by two open mouths. They are telling him off. He deserves it. He's fooling around. At this point if Ali thinks he's fooling Frazier, he has the cards upside down. He is fooling himself. My notes tell me that the fight is even, four to four, but believe me, the third, fourth, and this last round, were giveaways by Ali. In each of these rounds he invited Joe to come and punch, Joe did, and Ali did nothing in return. Joe is obviously still strong enough to *take* some of the remaining rounds on his own, if not all of them. It looks as if Ali's choice of patterns has failed.

Of course, every time Ali comes back with quick moves, jabs and combinations, he shows his physical superiority. What bothers me is that Frazier is showing the confidence *and* the will.

The bell announces round nine.

Ali circles Frazier. Frazier misses a left hook and a right. Ali is moving beautifully again. He looks like he believes he has found his "second wind."

A jab by Ali, another one. Ali follows with a jab, a right and a snappy left hook. Every jab hits Frazier who still laughs. Joe trails Ali closely. Ali snaps a left jab, turns to a left-handed stance and jabs with his right. Ali comes right back with a one–two combination. Now steps back calmly.

I don't know what to make of Ali now. He seems like the old Ali. He connects again with his left. Then Ali pushes Frazier back. What? Yes, that's right he just pushed the Machine back. Ali hits Frazier with a right. Frazier comes back with a jab and a right cross. They are now in the middle of the ring and they exchange blows. Man-to-man. Ali is the first one to step out of the short exchange. Frazier waves with his gloves at Ali to come back in close. Ali answers with a jab. Frazier comes running to Ali, and Ali stops him coming in with a stiff left jab, a perfect punch which can hurt as much as a good right cross. There is the bell. The fight is completely turned around. Ali won this round big, his best since the second.

One thing is clear to me now. I can't see how Frazier can win this fight. Ali just proved that when he wants, he can outmaneuver Joe. When they both are looking good, one can see Ali is the better man. But, one other thing is conclusively clear. Ali doesn't have full confidence. For if he does, why doesn't he force himself to try what he did in round nine more consistently? He is inconsistent, because he has no confidence. Either he is afraid of getting tired or afraid that if he takes more chances, he could get nailed by Frazier's left hook.

Meanwhile, Frazier seems to maintain the same type of pressure he's been putting on since the first second of fighting. When Ali was fresh, Joe was fresh. But now, the pace has slowed them a little. That's why when Ali stops fooling around in the ropes and throws punches, Frazier seems uneasy. At times, when Ali punches and moves, he makes Joe look like an amateur.

The gong says round ten.

Ali comes out and moves to his left. Joe throws a wild right that misses Ali. Now Ali moves to the center of the ring. Joe meets him. Ali moves back toward that spot, to his cursed spot.

Joe begins his work again. He is throwing fewer punches than before, but he's making more contact. A wicked left hook lands on Ali's body. A right takes Ali on his forehead. He is still there as if nothing is happening. He seems to be resting, which means he's thinking of giving this round away too. That's the beginning of corruption in a champ. My notes say that Ali is ahead by one round. If he presents Frazier with this round, it will be an even fight. At least, in my notes.

Ali has his own plan worked out. This man is using, in my opinion, wrong tactics, wrong patterns. Every change he makes is detrimental to him. When he tries to change, he loses his quality.

Undoubtedly, Ali's actions are encouraging to Joe. Every time Ali changes his pattern, Frazier's confidence builds. It's simple to understand. Ali is giving Frazier credit for too much complexity. He thinks if he shifts his pattern, Frazier will be confused. But Frazier just thinks Ali is getting dumb under the pressure. Joe just gets faster and stronger while Ali provides the ingredients.

Twenty seconds to go in this round and Ali has moved from one corner to the other, he has been on each set of ropes. Now he is to my far left, near his corner, northeast side of the Garden. He bobs and weaves under every single punch Frazier throws. He pulls away. Frazier misses again.

Frazier stops. He thinks, extends his left hand until it touches Ali, feints with his right and comes back with a vicious left hook. Misses. Goes back. Ali bends. Joe throws an uppercut. Misses. Ali throws one . . . two . . . three jabs. Hits. Comes back with a left–right combination of his own. Misses. Frazier throws a chopping right, comes back with a wicked left hook. Misses. The bell. This action by Ali took place in the last twenty to twenty-five seconds. But for two and a half minutes Frazier was chasing and Ali was going back *doing nothing*. Frazier missed a lot, but he was *doing something*. So my notes tell me that if the fight had been a ten-rounder, I would have scored it a draw.

However, I think that Ali turned the fight around in those last twenty seconds. When he stopped in his corner and concentrated on the defense, he made Joe miss ninety percent of his punches. When he decided to punch, he landed ninety percent of the time. Of course, by now, nothing is going to discourage Joe, but it might give Ali some support for his otherwise dubious performance.

Since the beginning, the fight has been in Ali's hands. He can win it or lose it himself. No matter what Frazier does, Ali has command. So far we have seen Frazier's consistent pattern and Ali's various ones. With the different transformations this fight has gone through, with Ali's performance averaging perhaps a poor forty percent, with some of the shots that have landed on Ali's face, the fight is close.

The buzzer disturbs my thoughts. Now the bell. It is round eleven. The next five rounds are the most important ones. If Ali continues to do what he did at the end of round ten, he can even knock Frazier out. But, his damn legs are leading him to the ropes again. Again! Frazier doesn't mind. He walks comfortably toward Ali.

I'm mad. What is he doing? Is he punchy? He had the fight won again in the final seconds of the tenth, and now he's spoiling it once more, staying up against the ropes with his back, shifting his face from one side to the other.

A left hook hits Ali!

Ali's legs shake. He was tagged! That was to the button. Ali can't control his weak legs. Frazier goes to the attack. He's hitting Ali's body with some vicious punches. A right to the body, a left to the body, now Frazier pushes Ali against the ropes.

Another sinful left hook!

Ali's legs buckle. He's at the edge of going to the canvas. His eyes are glassy. He has never been hurt this bad before in his entire career. He looks tired, disgusted, surprised, almost defeated. I don't know what's keeping him on his feet. Friends, Ali has guts. He has as much balls as Frazier. Believe me. I have never seen Frazier hurt this much. When Bonavena hurt him in their first fight, it was not as bad as the condition Ali is now in.

Ali's legs seem to be protesting. They can't carry the weight of his body too much longer. Ali's will is struggling to keep him on his feet. Frazier is punching. Frazier's muscles are forcing the arms to move faster, stronger. I can see it on his face.

Ali gets off of the ropes and we can all see that his legs are still weak. Strength keeps them from total collapse. Frazier has become a ferocious animal, a bear sending his claws in for the kill.

Yet Ali still plays games. He is a magician who will not let go of the cards. He pretends to be worse than he really is. He makes believe that he's going to fall. Frazier keeps coming. The bell. Bundini is up, outside the ring throwing water at Ali who walks slowly to his corner. Water splashes some of the newsmen at ringside. Bundini's man is hurt.

Ali slumps on the stool. Dundee works on his weak legs. Bundini pours water over Ali's head and back. Dundee and Bundini are both hurt. Bundini, surely, got hit with the same punches Ali got hit with.

A betrayal occurred when Ali got hit with those wicked shots. Ali's physical mechanism doublecrossed his mind. I'm very much inclined to believe that the three-and-a-half-year inactivity did in fact affect Ali's body performance. Ali's eyes saw both of Frazier's deadly hooks start, saw them from the beginning. Both hooks were extremely hard. Both slow, wild, telegraphed. Ali's mind said to his body: "Move." The body answered: "I can't." With that answer, his quick mind provided an alternative; it resisted the impact. Ali's courage kept the body from crumbling away. That was why he didn't go down. Could that courage which *kept* him on his feet be consistent enough to help his will *win* the fight?

My notes say that Ali is behind technically and my mind tells me that he is far behind psychologically. Ali might come back in the next round to try to vindicate himself. I hope not. He could get flattened. No emotion please. Be cool.

Round twelve just began.

Round twelve finds Ali searching for answers. He had a minute to recover from the beating he got in the previous round. On the stool he *saw* better what had happened to him. I think he's testing his legs. He moves to his left, now to his right. Frazier resumes the attack. Frazier pins Ali against the ropes once again. Ali keeps his right hand close to his cheek. He doesn't want to catch any more of those savage hooks on his chin. He is not showing it, but I know he is worried. He is even afraid to throw punches. He doesn't want to expose his chin to Joe's hooks.

Seems to me that Ali has chosen defeat as a reality tonight. He is doing it with class; he is making the choice Ché Guevara made; the Kennedys made; Martin Luther King; Malcolm X; Benny Kid Paret. These men didn't purposely go to be killed in the particular place or day that they died; they just got killed. And each of these men had a distinct way of dying. Each of them died being a *man*. Paret and Bobby Kennedy smiled; King and Malcolm and John Kennedy had ironic looks. It was as if they'd fooled that part of the world which is rotten.

Ali has that sign. He's going to get beat, but with class. It'll be his choice, not Frazier's. Of course, that's his confidence talking. Yet sometimes when confidence lies positively it can convince the will. With Ali, of course, this could be a complicated situation.

Ali's confidence could believe it is the boss. It might have conversations with his will. "Mister Will," confidence could say, "I'm going to lie about us, I want those lies to be true."

So Mr. Will begins to work, to fight. Many times, they come out victorious.

Round twelve dies. It took a little of Ali with it.

Let me remind you. Ali has the physical ability to beat this man. He is like the 155 mm cannon loaded with shells, but with no one to pull the string. D'Amato used to tell me when I committed a stupid mistake inside the ring: "José, a stupid man could be forgiven for his stupidity; a smart man who doesn't use his intelligence shouldn't."

The bell. For those of you who are superstitious, for those builders who raise towers and jump from the twelfth to the fourteenth floor, this is round thirteen. It is for poor Ali too.

After his big ninth round, Ali has lost three consecutive rounds. If he wants to impress the three officials who will decide this fight, if both fighters are still walking straight after the fifteenth round, he better start doing something now.

And I don't mean *that!* He is on the ropes again. Frazier now looks like a man who began pushing a loaded truck uphill a long thirty-six minutes ago and his energy is threatening to give out. At the top of the hill is two and a half million dollars in loot. Thirty-one real tough men have tried before and each one has failed. It is not a game, it's serious business.

His arms are tired, his legs weigh two hundred pounds each, his lungs want everyone to stop breathing so he can get *all* the oxygen. Joe Frazier doesn't even stop now to look how far he is from the loot. He is going to find the strength someplace. It could be in a place beyond all his past capacities.

That's the way Frazier is punching now. His body burns with fire, his blood boils. Every organ of his body works for Joe. He might retire after this match. It could be his last fight and Joe is not going to let the "phony" in front of him tarnish his unblemished record. He is fighting with ego, with selfishness, with sadism. He's going to push the truck all the way up there. Even if he has to die to do it. Ladies and gentlemen, you can't ask for more. This is the will to win at its maximum posture.

Not once did I look at the clock. So the bell catches me listening to the murmur of Ali's constituency, the noise of Frazier's crowd.

This is the fourth round in a row that Ali has failed to win. I see no reason why he should come out and try harder in the next two. His ego, his machismo is not working for him. I think he's going to concentrate on going the limit. That's right. Ali is going to be a hard man to hit clean from now on. Every little energy he has is going to be put into one place: defense.

Sometimes, when I was in a tough spot in regard to my boxing training, I used to sleep. That was my way of escaping the real world. I feel that way now. I'm sleepy.

The fucking bell awakens me. It's, for those who are still counting, the fourteenth.

Ali is pulled again by the magnet of the ropes. The power of the magnet seems to increase on his body which in turn pulls in Frazier. And Frazier swings. Misses. Frazier swings again. Misses. Wait a minute! What's going on? Ali moves out and now he is the one doing the swinging. Connects. Swings again with a vicious left hook to Frazier's head. A right. He pushes Joe back and hits him with a one–two combination. Wow!

It seems as if this supreme effort is his alternative. He is using those mysterious forces. I can't explain it any other way. Ali is moving again.

He slides to his left and shoots a left jab. He changes to southpaw and jabs with his right. Comes back with a long left hook that passes over Frazier's moving head. I don't know if Joe is surprised, but I am. I think there is only one explanation for what's happening in the ring now. Ali, thinking that the pace was too fast, laid on the ropes for the last four rounds to see if Joe could punch himself out. At the same time he was saving energy for the last two rounds.

He explodes now. He looks like a new man. But he could be faking. The punches could be empty. I hope not. He throws a jab, another one, follows them with a right. He's not smiling. He knows that his psychology inside the ring has not been working against Joe. So he is all business now.

Joe still tries to connect but in vain. Ali has become a moving target once more. Of course, he's not moving fast, but Frazier is not charging fast either.

That was the bell and Ali *could* have a chance to pull through this fight. I have it eight rounds to six with Joe ahead, but I found myself cursing at Ali and in my pad I have round ten circled with a question mark. Any one of the three officials could have given it to Ali. With that possibility in mind, the fight could be seven to seven, with round fifteen the decisive one. If that's a fact, this is a very interesting fight. A great fight.

Expectation is still the word to use to describe the excited crowd. No one is sure who is ahead. Some say Ali, some say Frazier, but nobody is yelling one-sided.

Last round?

They are tired. Mercante is tired. The crowd is tired. I am tired. How much can the crowd do for their favorite? How much can I do for Ali? Maybe no waves can penetrate the root of the fighters. They have to stop outside waves. Their forces can't permit any outside interference.

Friends, Frazier is ready. He's walking a little faster, with more conviction in his steps. Frazier is getting ready to go beyond the tiredness of human flesh, beyond the function of the muscles. Joe Frazier has the attitude of a Trujillo, Duvalier, Franco. Yes, Joe is a dictator who tells his subordinates what to do. He is telling his hands, his legs, his heart and his lungs, that they must respect his mandate that they are going to withstand every imposition he might coerce on them. That's that.

And Ali, what is Ali? Some kind of crazy democrat? I have to think about that. Into the fifteenth!

Ali is moving toward his corner with Joe almost on top of him. Ali moves to his left. He moves now to the center of the ring. He moves straight back to the south side of the ring between his corner and the northwest corner. He moves his left foot back. Joe starts a left hook. He leaps with it. Ali is moving his head back slowly and not looking at Frazier. The left hook is reaching Ali's jaw. Too late. Ali sees it at contact. Ali's neck snaps to his left. Explosion. One million ants enter his body! As soon as they get in, they get out. Ali is not aware that his legs are folding under him. His eyes are closed momentarily. His body is falling fast. He's flat on his back. His joints are being moved by the nerves, without any message from the consciousness.

One second has passed and Ali's eyes are trying to focus desperately.

If he stays down every patriotic sportswriter will have a word to describe Ali: coward.

The referee says three and Ali is up. He is going to fight back. He walks toward Joe with a swollen jaw, the right side of his face distorted with the power of Joe's malevolent left hook. Frazier attacks. He just won the fight. The damage has been irreparable. The impact of that blow took everything Ali had left. He is there strictly to finish the fight on his own two feet.

Ali's magic didn't work. Ali's magic is honest. Ali's magic now works detached from Ali's other ingredients. Ali's magic is the only ingredient in Ali's boxing qualities that tells the truth. And Ali's magic says that when two great black fighters have a serious conflict, the one to win is he who deserves to win.

Tonight, in fact *now*, as Johnny Addie announces the decision of the two judges and the referee—all voted for Joe—Mr. Frazier deserved to win. Long live Ali's magic conviction.

CHAPTER 18

Two days ago, Monday, June 28, 1971, I looked at the back cover of the *New York Daily News* and saw a smiling face. It was Muhammad Ali's. The big letters said: "ALI WINS DECISION." A subtitle says: "Court Votes 8–0 to Kayo Draft Rap."

Inside, the *News'* two oldest sports columnists, Dick Young and Gene Ward, are sad when they mention Ali's triumph. Of all the sportswriters in New York, Young and Ward are the ones who consistently had adverse criticism for Ali.

Reluctantly, Ward accepts the decision of those eight Supreme Court judges who concluded Ali was not a draft dodger. Young goes to the New York Mets baseball team and discusses the decision with them.

I look at the situation with the eyes of a fighter.

Undoubtedly, Ali has scored the biggest triumph of his life. (My mother just called to find out how my book was going, and said: "Tell Ali that I'm happier now than the night he won the championship from Liston.") The triumph, of course, was a victory for American justice rather than for Ali himself. In other words, Ali's victory helps to bring justice to America, and that's a rather tremendous conquest.

Americans who made the world safe for democracy over the protest of Quakers in World War I, must now make Southeast Asia safe over the protests of the Black Muslims and the courts have finally given the same protection to the Muslims that they gave to the Quakers.

On July 26, Ali is fighting ex-sparring partner and stablemate Johnny Ellis in the Astrodome in Houston. And the Supreme Court decision might have an effect on Ali's future performances.

Today, three months and twenty-two days after being beaten by Joe Frazier, Ali is beginning to do what he should have done after the Quarry fight. He is going to take, so he says, a few fights, two or three, before getting into a ring with Frazier again.

The reason should be a simple one. Ali is in search of something he lost. That something could be confidence. Listening to him after the fight, he said he trained hard, but not hard enough; he said that laying against the ropes was a bad mistake, but that he felt Frazier would punch himself out. So, Muhammad Ali is becoming rational where he used to depend on intuition. He's going to begin now, in the middle months of this year, to prepare for the second fight with Frazier early next year.

But what will happen if they—Ali and Frazier—square off against each other again?

Frazier spent a couple of weeks in the hospital in Philadelphia and is now on European tour with his band. I've seen him on a couple of TV shows singing. Ali, until he signed to fight Ellis, was back on the road making speeches at colleges. In fact, Ali has become in defeat, a very important man. The loss seems to have given him more popularity in this country. Now the Supreme Court decision comes. He wins a battle by a margin that boxing never gave him. Eight-to-zero.

This new popularity may make Ali too happy. His court victory has been the achievement of his life. Nothing could make

Ali feel better, even winning back the title. So Ali, whom I now pick to win a return bout, could nonetheless find himself more contented with these major legal victories than a simple ring victory. Frazier, who put a maximum of pressure in his last fight, but not much desire in his punching, was affected too by the cost of his victory which I believe used up much of his remaining desire.

We find here, then, two men who are, in effect, en route to a relative deterioration from their maximum. But, say, for example, that they both lose their desire at a similar rate. Who would be most affected?

Ali depends on speed and coordination; he depends on confidence and will. Frazier depends on the pressure he uses, on the quantity of punches; on his will, toughness and refusal to step back. He also counts on his very strong left hooks.

The last things fighters lose are strength and punching power. These are flesh powers. One may hit the target a little slower, but the punch will be there.

Ali doesn't punch strongly and has never used his strength to beat an opponent. So once his speed of hand and foot slows, he's in serious trouble. His punches won't hurt, and his jaw may catch a few more of those left hooks that Frazier loves to wing.

Frazier will have the strength and the wallop. He is, of course, an easy man to figure out. He beat Ali exactly the way he said he would over and over again before the fight. He is like an open book. A true machine. That makes Frazier the sure winner if neither has high motivation for this next fight. But, another possibility is that Ali might *really* make up his mind to make the Ali–Frazier match his last one and concentrate everything.

Then Ali might find out that it was his mistakes, instead of Frazier's virtues, which caused his defeat. So he might concentrate on the weaknesses of the Dictator next time.

Since he no longer can count on his magic (with Frazier at least), Ali might begin to look for a pugilistic rather than a magical solution. I think he has realized that it was not what Frazier did, but what he didn't do, which provided him with his first defeat.

Strangely, Frazier's strongest motivation for a future Ali–Frazier match, should be his past victory. Ali's motivation should be his defeat. It is not a paradox; it is that Muhammad Ali can't begin to measure the complexities of his future. Ali has come toward a choice. He's a popular man today in America. He could become, with a victory over Frazier, a national hero to many who do not yet even wish to respect him. If his ego or his professional vanity is aware of this dimension, then Ali could produce his own motivation. Never will a fighter have a larger psychological purse depending on a ring victory. A distinguished career *outside* the ring could then lie ahead of him, an enormous career as leader of his people.

But, of course, we never know if the real Muhammad Ali will ever stand up.

"When I die," he said the other day in an upstate New York College, "I want my tombstone to read: 'No fooling! No fooling. But the name's been changed to protect the innocent.' "

What an epitaph!

EPILOGUE
BY
BUDD SCHULBERG

Why are so many writers drawn to prizefighting and fighters? In England, essayists, poets and novelists like William Hazlitt, Lord Byron and Conan Doyle chummed with the bareknuckle marvels, sparred with them and wrote vividly about them. And in America there is an impressive body of work on the subject of the Manly Art and the manly artists. Jack London not only wrote the superb short stories "A Piece of Steak" and "The Mexican" and a couple of boxing novels, he also took time from his fiction to cover the big fights of his day for the *New York Tribune*. In his path came Ernest Hemingway, Joseph Moncure March, Ring and John Lardner, Nelson Algren, Norman Mailer and your epilogist. All of them were trying to do more than describe a physical, even a brutal event. They saw the contest between two men as transcending cruel hand-to-hand combat. They saw it as metaphor in motion, as basic combat elevated to the stage of a morality play. I have heard the Hemingways, the Mailers, and the Algrens—in fact all of us who find method and meaning in The Sweet Science—put down as would-be tough guys, literary know-nothings who get our jollies from hanging in with pugs and describing the lumps they inflict on each other. We're sometimes accused of being frustrated prizefighters ourselves. What the critics fail to understand is that while boxing may be the most sadistic of all our sports, it is also the most intellectual. Among amateurs and unsophisticated preliminary boys you may see fighters who stand there in their basic ignorance and simply hit or get hit. But that, as Joe Torres explains so lucidly in this welcome first book, is exactly what the art of boxing refutes.

Boxing is psychology. Boxing is outguessing which means outthinking your opponent. Boxing is a game of chess in which your head and torso, like that of your opponent, becomes the board upon which you play. Or to put it another way, football buffs enjoy trying to out-quarterback the quarterback, to pick with him the play he will call next and to anticipate the deception with which he carries out his strategy. But in the ring, the fighter must be his own quarterback, and must not only call the plays but act as his own front-line, his own line-backer, his own pass-defense. If you can conceive of a one-man football team you will appreciate some of the tactical, psychological and emotional as well as physical problems of a first-rate fighter.

Do you begin to understand what Nelson, or Norman and I see in boxing? Then you will be ready to accept our conviction that fighters tend to be not the most brutalized of our athletes but the most sensitive and intelligent. I remember being introduced to the Dodgers in Spring training when only Carl Erskins had an inkling as to who I was. Nor do I think any published writer would have fared any better. *Writers*—said their sullen, preoccupied eyes—*who needs 'em?* Baseball players as a rule tend to be what the general public might expect of men who fight for money. But over the years I have noticed that just as writers are drawn to fighters, the reverse is also true. I am not saying that

every boxer is a Gene Tunney who likes to take walks with Bernard Shaw. But all my life I have noticed how fighters respond to writers, even if they barely recognize their names, even if they never read their books, or any books. It is easy for writers and fighters to establish a common meeting ground. Neither one has a team to lean on or mates with whom to share the trials of success and failure. Both must draw on their innermost resources and create from their personal experiences something that is not only entertaining but meaningful and winning in the deepest sense. Both of them must conquer their fears, transform their weaknesses into strengths. And both of them must learn to absorb punishment, standing up to the left jabs and the hard right hands of their critics. I remember talking about this with Rocky Marciano when he was preparing for his final title defense against Archie Moore. Rocky wasn't a reader but again and again he would ask me about the process of writing. I felt at home with him in his remote farmhouse because it was exactly the kind of place Norman, or Pete Hamill or any other practicing writer would go to get a job of work done.

So while it may be unique, it isn't the least surprising that José Torres, former Light Heavyweight Champion of the World, has turned in his boxing gloves for a portable typewriter. It is a notorious fact that after a fighter wins a world title he is apt to fall into bad company who will lead him astray. Well, José, instead of swinging with the boys of Bachelors III, fell in with Mailer, Hamill, George Plimpton and some other word-men and I doubt if he was ever again as good a fighter as he was the night he demolished the educated defense of Willie The Wisp Pastrano. Because José had other things on his mind now. He began to analyze writers as he had those tough opponents—Benny Paret, Bobo Olson, Dick Tiger—in the ring. He became a columnist for the *New York Post*, fighting his way up from preliminary ranks

to main events. He was frightened as all writers are frightened, but he conquered his fear. When he tells you in this book about fear in the dressing room, giving you an inside picture of the fighter's psyche you may never have had before, or when he is discussing the genius and the fears of his friend Muhammad Ali, he is obviously not only writing about boxing, he is talking about writing, since at their best both mediums demand the same concentration, self-discipline and the aspiration of art.

So as he climbs through the rope to hit us a very clean shot with his first published book, let's hear it for José "Chequi" Torres, who's proved what we always have believed: great fighters are basically frustrated writers. And now that the pride of Ponce has proved he can go the distance in a larger ring without ropes, strike *frustrated*. Young Mr. Torres's publishing record now reads: Won—1; Lost—0.

Could his old fight manager Norman Mailer or his old literary advisor Cus D'Amato ask more of their talented protégé? From *Boxing Illustrated* to the *New York Times Book Review*, he's made a graceful transition. Now the bell is ringing for Book 2, Chequi! Punch in there, and as every honest writer and fighter knows he must, continue to draw on the qualities that make a champion—intelligence, emotional stamina, one's artful best. And if Mailer, D'Amato and I, a motley trio indeed, were to call out any last minute literary advice from your corner, it could not be put more succinctly or poetically than "Float like a butterfly, sting like a bee." From Homer to Hemingway, and from Tacitus to Torres, that's what it's all about.